The Little Blue Book Of Selling

By John Brentlinger

Foreword by David Thomas

THE LITTLE BLUE BOOK OF SELLING

Copyright 2002
By John D. Brentlinger

All rights reserved. No part of this publication may be used or reproduced in any form without the written consent of the author. Exceptions include any salesperson who needs to jot down notes on the back of his/her hand for use during the sales process; sales managers who are not prepared for Monday morning sales meetings, and third year law students for finals.

© Land's End, Inc. Used with permission.

© Blockbuster. Used with permission.

The author can be reached:
By telephone at: 1.800.380.3040
E-mail: littlebluebookofselling@hotmail.com

ISBN: 0-9759027-0-9 PRINTED IN U.S.A.

To my wife, Jan, who for thirty-one years
has patiently allowed me to march
to the beat of a
different drummer,
this book is affectionately dedicated.

This book has been written for a specific group of people — those brave men and women who sell cars for a living.

They work long hours, and sacrifice family time and important events to work a schedule that most salespeople would not even attempt.

The automotive industry is the largest, greatest, most necessary business in the world. Have you noticed? We don't walk much anymore. We drive.

And you would think that the people who sell these products would be among the most respected, highest paid, well-rounded salespeople in the world.

Well, they can be. I hope this little book helps.

Table Of Contents

Always respect your superiors,
if you have any.
— Mark Twain

Foreword

After twenty years and some 5000 sales later, I finally found someone who tells it like it is! If I had read this book twenty years ago, I could be retired and on the golf course.

Whether you are selling cars, computers, real estate or widgets, this book empowers you to understand the customer and what they really want, in just a matter of routine steps in closing sales. John Brentlinger hits the mark in helping you connect with your customers. When they trust and respect you, they will buy from you.

John is not just a motivational speaker, but a factual teacher of the most successful sales strategy I know. I have adopted this philosophy at my dealerships. By using these tips and techniques you will sell more, make more money and most importantly, enjoy your career more.

David Thomas
David Thomas Auto Group
Dallas, Texas

Preface

In every bookstore in the country, there are countless books on selling. The authors' names are familiar to almost everyone in sales. Some names are more familiar than others, and if you purchase many books, tapes, or CD's on selling, you can still hear the names and learn most of their techniques. There are many speakers and salespeople who still use these same, old, stale sales techniques, and who still get paid for teaching them.

The problem with these old sales techniques is, even though prospects know them, the majority of salespeople still use them. By the time you get to use one of these old, outdated techniques on your prospect, the prospect has probably heard it ten times in the last month.

Most books on selling are heavy on technique and light on concepts. Most sales training seems to be quick fix, snake oil, manipulative and scheming. And if it seems that way, then maybe it is. A great deal of sales training is so systematized, so structured, and so confining, that it becomes difficult to understand and put into practice.

Today there are more books on selling than at any time in history. Yet across the nation, sales turnover is at an all time high, and our personal discontent with how we are treated almost every time we try to buy something is even higher.

The fact is that old, outdated methods of sales training just are not working with today's educated, intelligent, well-trained customers.

Most sales training today is technical training; how to close, how to ask positive questions, how to control the sale; how to get information from the prospect, and etcetera. But since most of that training is based on old information, that sort of selling offends today's prospects.

What is needed is conceptual training. Conceptual training focuses on the prospect and why they buy, what they want, what they need, and how they want to be treated. Conceptual training focuses on people skills and on what motivates buyers to buy or not buy. Conceptual training is the key to selling more, and helping more prospects get what they want.

Conceptual selling is the missing link in the automobile business. It is the key to selling more cars, retaining better salespeople, and keeping a loyal customer base. Technical training and massive amounts of product knowledge simply have not worked to retain good salespeople and keep loyal customers. Conceptual selling, which places the wants and needs of the customer first, is the key to success in the car business today.

Selling cars is front line selling. Automobile salespeople are the infantry of the sales world. They are in the trenches everyday, they see good, qualified prospects on a daily basis, and they must utilize their skills constantly if they are to succeed. Most sales systems don't really address the everyday issues of front line selling. This little book does just that.

The chapters are brief. The subjects are common sense and simple. The chapters are meant to stand alone. You can pick up the book, read one chapter and go immediately to a prospect and practice what you just read. There are no systems to memorize, no charts to carry; just some simple, easy, important ways to deal with the prospects you see every day.

If you bought this little book to learn new secrets, or some great new sales technique or some smack down closes, you probably should return the book immediately; maybe exchange it for one titled something like, "How to Control Prospects," "How to Get Prospects to do Anything You Want Them To," "How to get them to Buy What You Want to Sell," and yada yada yada.

But, if you bought this book because you are struggling to sell, because you have tried the old techniques for years and found them not to work, or if you just want to be more of a consultant to your customer and help them get what they want and need, this may be your book.

Selling is not manipulation, twisting arms, or using psychology to get people to buy things they don't want, don't need or can't afford.

Selling is helping prospects discover what they really want, truly need, what they are willing to pay to get it, and then helping them get it.

If you can take the simple tips in this little book, and execute them on a daily basis with real prospects, you will sell more, make more, help more people, and do it without going crazy in the process.

This is not another "How To" book on selling. This is a "How To Be" book on selling. In selling, who we are speaks much louder than what we say.

John Brentlinger
August, 2002

Introduction

There is an old Aesop's fable which goes something like this:

Once upon a time there was a farmer who owned a goose which laid every day one golden egg. For a while, the farmer and his wife were content with one golden egg a day.

But after a while, their greed got the better of them, and supposing that the goose contained the magic of making gold inside, they killed the goose to get to the good stuff.

To their surprise, the inside of the goose was no different than the other geese. The foolish pair, hoping to become rich all at once, deprived themselves of the daily gain of which they were already assured.

There is a direct analogy between this old fable, and the business of selling cars.

> The secret to success in the car business is in the daily application of listening, discovering real wants and true needs, finding out what the prospect is willing to pay, and then selling them what they really want, and truly need at the price they want to pay. It is that simple.

That process is the goose that lays the golden egg.

This book is not an elegant treatise on some new selling system. It is not meant as some great new selling technique. It is simply a gentle reminder that if we listen more to the prospect, if we seek to understand the three things most important to the customer, their wants, needs and budget, and if we are willing to focus on the prospect instead of our commission, then we cannot help but sell more.

The foundation of this little book is this:

For the customer, their three greatest concepts are their wants, their needs, and their budget, in that order.

If you can discover what those three things are, you will have no trouble doubling or tripling your sales.

The reverse is also true.

If you forget those three things which are so important to the customer, if you focus on your wants, your needs, and your commission, you will continually struggle to maintain average sales.

The choice is yours.

Chapter One

To The Reader

There are salespeople who break every rule in this book and still make a lot of money. But they are the exception, not the rule. They are not like the rest of us. The rest of us need good people skills and polite manners.

There are other salespeople who do by nature the things contained in this book. They just naturally sell and make a great deal of money. But they are the exception, not the rule. They are not like the rest of us. The rest of us need to learn good people skills and polite manners because for most of us, these things do not come naturally.

So we have to work at it.

This book is not for the salespeople who break all the rules or for the salespeople who are just naturally great. This book is for the other 99 percent of us who still have to work for everything we get.

> God gives every bird his food, but He does not throw it into the nest.
>
> — C.H. Spurgeon

Chapter Two

Prospects Have More Reasons To Buy Than We Do To Sell

Why do we sell? That's easy, because we need the money. Period. That is our one reason for selling. Every other reason we tell ourselves revolves around the money. And there is nothing wrong with that. But that is why we sell. And the prospect knows that. There is nothing wrong with that either. Both the prospect and the salesperson go to work every day for the same reason. It's the money. And while every prospect may not be a salesperson, the company they work for must provide goods or services at a profit. No profit, no job, no business.

Think about the mental process you go through before you buy something. First, you must justify in your mind that you need a new "whatever." You justify your need with statements and thoughts to yourself like, "the old one is worn out, the paint is fading, the model is outdated, it's boring, it won't get the job done anymore, it looks bad, it sounds bad, the new ones have more pep, the new ones are more economical, the new ones look nicer, the old one is hard to start, not reliable, the wife makes fun of it, the kids laugh at it, it is time for a new one."

Those are just some of the things we tell ourselves. Once we have convinced ourselves, then we begin to justify it to our spouse, because our spouse has reasons also. Once our spouse buys in on it, then we really get serious. We look through the paper, we search the Internet, the yellow pages, the magazines, and we begin to collect clear, objective reasons why the old one is not good enough.

And at some invisible point in the process, the new one becomes a down-right necessity, and the old one becomes a liability. It is at this point that we begin to consider ways to move heaven and earth to find the money to pay for the new one. We cut expenses, we put off another project, we pick up some spare income, and we find a way to buy something which by now, we have convinced ourselves that we absolutely cannot live without. With that frame of mind, we get into the car and we go look for the object of our desire.

Your attention please: It is exactly this state of mind that your prospects are in when they first drive on your lot or walk in your showroom.

Now wouldn't it be a good idea to greet the prospect sincerely, warmly and kindly, and then just be quiet for the next twenty minutes while they tell you all their reasons for buying? And maybe go one step further and let them tell you everything before you start with the meet & greet, qualify, present, close thing.

Maybe we should save the dynamic selling tactics, the trial closes, the qualifying questions for later, much later. How about we just ask questions, listen for the answers and stop with the yada, yada, yada? Because at this point, the prospect has already sold themselves, the husband, the wife, the kids, the friends and anyone else who will listen. ***The only one who doesn't know that they are already sold is the salesperson.***

> Because we are salespeople, we think that we need to sell the prospect on a new vehicle. We don't. They've already sold themselves. All we have to do is find out what they really want, truly need and how much they are willing to pay to get it.

It really is that simple.

We may as well face the truth: the old school way of selling drives away 3 out of 4 prospects. We are at best only selling 1 out of 4, when if we just gave them a chance to tell their story, to tell us what they want and why, to tell us what they need and why; to tell us how much they want to spend and why; but no, we need to interrupt, to trial close, to demonstrate, to test drive, to do features and benefits and in doing that, we drive them away. No sale, no commission. All we had to do was let them tell their story, then help them get ***what they had already decided to buy.***

The only thing they need the salesperson for is to help them get what they want.

Prospects have more reasons to buy than we do to sell. About all we have to do is to listen to their story, then help them get what they have already decided to buy.

How hard is that?

Chapter Three

Stop Asking For Their Name And Number

Consider the following scenario: a man is walking down the street. He sees an attractive woman walking towards him. The man rushes up to the woman, stops right in front of her and says, “Hi, my name is Bob, could I get your name and number?”

Now there are only about 50 reasons why that scenario is rude, improper, cold, impolite, unfair and threatening. But if we think about it, isn’t that what happens to most prospects on your lot in their first sixty seconds at your dealership?

Prospect walks into your showroom and is greeted immediately by a stranger with a big grin, an outstretched hand and the proverbial, “Hi, my name is Bob, what’s yours?”

It is just like the initial scenario, and for the prospect it does not compute. Why on earth should the prospect give their name and number to a perfect stranger? As a salesperson, you may not like that question, but then consider yourself as a prospect. You buy things. Do **you** give your name and number to every salesperson who asks you for it? Do **you** listen patiently to the telephone solicitors when **you** are having dinner with your family? Or as a prospect, do you consider those calls, and requests for information as intrusive?

There will be a point in the sales process where you are allowed to politely ask the prospect's name. You'll know when you have reached that point. Their phone number is not yet necessary, unless they offer it to you first. You do not need their phone number to help them discover what they really want, truly need and what they are willing to spend. So, practice. ***Don't kill the goose.*** Stop expecting to get that information in the first few minutes of the selling process.

It is when the prospect sees you as being sincerely interested in their wants that they will freely give you information which most of us still consider to be private.

When the prospect trusts you enough to give you their name and number, only then do you have a chance at getting the sale anyway. If they will not give you their name and number, it is a sign that you have not yet earned their trust. And that is not their fault. It is yours.

And of course, if they don't trust you, they won't buy anyway. So don't ask for their name and number. Just be the kind of salesperson who earns their trust, who asks questions, who listens, and who sincerely wants to help them get what they really want, truly need and can afford. If you do that, they will offer their name and number freely. And they will buy from you, because you earned their trust.

P.S. When they do give you their name, don't be silly with it. I know that Dale Carnegie said that a person's name to them is the sweetest music on earth, and all that stuff, and it could be true.

But when you get their name, use it sincerely. Don't say, "Well, here's something to consider, Rodger, when your driving habits are important enough to you, Rodger, to consider this all wheel drive, Rodger...........and blah blah Rodger blah."

Please do not over use their name. It sounds silly and prospects know what you are doing and why you are doing it. Just be sincere.

By the way, just so you know, all of your commission is earned in the first five minutes of the sales process. If you mess up here, you're not going to recover. If you offend the prospect because of your approach, your behavior, your attempts to qualify them before they trust you, you are driving them to your competition. You may as well take them in a limo.

Chapter Four

Stop Closing

Prospects are ready for your closes. They are ready for your trial closes. They consider those old closes as high pressure. They consider them offensive. They do not like them. They do not appreciate them, and they do not think that those old, worn out closes are cute. And if you are the third dealership they have shopped that day, they have just heard the same closes, word for word, from the last two salespeople. That's why they didn't laugh when you tried to make the closes cute and funny.

To the prospect, the close is like a steel trap. If they answer it your way, they are somehow committed to buy. If they ignore it or object to it, they know that you will try harder in another minute or two with another close, so they prepare themselves to resist it.

A trial close adds fuel to the fire of an offended prospect.

A trial close pushes the prospect further from the sale.

A trial close means that you have not done your job of sincerely finding out what the prospect wants, why they want it, how bad they need it, what will happen if they don't get it, what they have done so far to find it, and what you can do to help them get it.

A strong armed close is another way of saying to the prospect, "I have not listened closely to what you want and need. I don't really care what you want and need. I need to make this sale so I am trying as hard as I can to get you to buy what I think you need. And if this close doesn't work, I know about a dozen more." That is what you are really saying to the prospect when you close early and often.

If you do your job properly, if you listen to the prospect, if you find out what they want, what they need, when they want and need it, what they are willing to pay to get it; if you just show sincere interest in them, you will have a chance to help them get what they want.

> If you show no sincere interest in them, no matter how great you think you are at closing, you have no chance of selling to the majority of your prospects.

So ask questions, listen to the answers, pay attention to them. And if you do this, *they will ask you if they can buy.* You won't need to learn any new closes, and you can forget the old ones that didn't work anyway.

Stop closing. Closes are excuses for salespeople who are not sincerely concerned about their prospects' needs, wants and budget. Closes are for salespeople who are more concerned about their commission check, rather than about helping the prospect get what they want and need, in the price range they can afford.

Stop closing. Just help your prospect get what they want.

Prospects don't buy because of how you phrase something, or because of some fancy schmancy close you heard at the last seminar.

All the bear trap closes in the world will never work with a prospect whose wants have been ignored by the salesperson.

Chapter Five

Start Opening

Okay, if we are going to stop closing, then we need to start opening.

Rule: every step in the selling process must lead openly to help the prospect discover what they want, need, and can afford.

In a closing oriented situation, every step in the sales process leads, funnel like, with an increasing series of traps, to force the prospect to say "yes" to what the salesperson wants to sell.

Can you recognize the adversarial position, the automatic tension, the mental warring and mind games which both parties must then play during the sales process which is weighted heavily on high handed closes?

Check the dictionary definition of the word, "close." The word means, "shut, not open; narrow, confining, restricted." To us as salespeople, the close has always meant, "I'm trying for the sale." To our prospects, the close sounds like the negative, harsh, icy cold snap of a steel trap closing tight. To the prospect it sounds like, "You're nailed, buddy."

If you want to sell more, if you want to sell 3 out of 4 instead of 1 out of 4, if you want to help them get what they want, need and will pay for, then you must keep all lines of communication open. Enough trial closes and the poor prospect learns not to say anything. If your concern is to genuinely help the prospect, and you do your job in helping them discover what they want and need, at some point, and we do not know where, they will make a decision to buy.

And I stress, we do not know exactly where or when this point is. And furthermore, it does not matter where or when this point is. It only matters to the prospect. It is their buying decision, not your selling decision.

Before you get to that point, you need to ask open questions, and listen to the answers the prospect gives you. You need to make sure that both you and the prospect are clear on where you are going and why, and you must make sure that the prospect feels that you are working **for** them.

Only when the lines of communication are open on both sides, only when there is a mutual transfer of sincere information, with you and the prospect being openly honest with each other, can the sales process be beneficial for both parties.

> The worst sort of sales situation is where the prospect is pressured into hiding information, not telling the whole truth, because they are afraid they will have to buy something they either do not want or cannot afford.

And the more they hide, cover up, and do not reveal their true wants and needs, the harder the salesperson tries to sell them something, anything, and it can turn out to be the wrong thing, at the wrong price, for the wrong reason. Both parties then feel cheated.

Consider the following paragraph from an Ohio Supreme Court Opinion, dated June 28, 2001:

> The car buying experience may be the most complicated mating dance in all of the animal world. It seems a given that both parties must engage in half-truths ("I don't know if I can afford this"), double meanings ("Let's see if we can make the numbers work"), semantic gymnastics ("Priced below invoice"), expressions of powerlessness ("Let me talk to my manager"/"Let me talk to my spouse"), and white lies ("I'm talking to someone at another dealership") before the relationship finally culminates in a deal.
>
> — 92 Ohio St.3d 327

Stop closing. Start opening. Open the lines of communication to the prospect. Open up with a sincere, simple, friendly greeting. Here's an idea, once you and the prospect are on speaking terms, why not say, "My job is to help you discover exactly what you want and need, in the price range you want to pay. I feel we can work together to make that happen. Does that sound okay to you?"

Openness, honesty, sincerity, friendliness, understanding, these are the keys which will help you stop closing and start opening.

Chapter Six

To Tell The Truth

You know, it might be wise to place the courtroom oath on our bathroom mirror, so that every morning before work, we could repeat it to ourselves:

> With my prospects today, I promise to tell the truth, the whole truth and nothing but the truth, so help me God.

Telling the whole truth to our prospects means that we just tell the truth. It means that we will not lie to our prospects.

Lies like, "You need to decide on this one today, I got three other people looking at it." Like, "Better make up your mind, I got a guy driving from Ft. Wayne to look at this baby." The really funny thing about those lies and others like them, is that if the prospect goes three or four places, they hear the same lies, often on the same day, from different salespeople. And of course they recognize the lies for what they are, not genuine, not real, not the truth.

I'm not trying to get preachy here. All I am saying is that if we are in the business to help people get what they want, and if we expect them to trust us, and if they are going to spend their money with us, they deserve up front honesty and sincerity.

And the more we strive for honesty and sincerity, the more we will sell, and the more referrals and repeat business we will get.

> Salespeople who lie won't get many referrals.

Like Mark Twain said, "If you tell the truth, you don't have to remember what you said."

Chapter Seven

People Buy For Their Reasons, Not Ours

If our foundation for selling is self-centered instead of prospect centered, if our focus is on our dealership, our products, our manager, our techniques, our training and our product knowledge, then our selling conversation will be focused on those things. If we focus on who we are, what we've done, how we've done it, what we have, what we can do, then the wants and needs of the prospect do not get addressed. We are too busy focusing on us. If we do not build our sales process around and upon the wants and needs of the prospect, then our foundation for selling is suspect.

But if we build our foundation for selling around the reasons the prospect has to buy, based on what they really want, truly need and are willing to pay for, then the prospect becomes the center of our sales process.

What are the prospect's reasons to buy? It depends on the prospect. Every prospect is different. Every prospect will have different reasons for buying. To us, the reasons may sound the same, but to the prospect, those reasons are personal and of utmost importance to them.

> When we, as the salespeople, start telling the prospect why they should buy, the prospect becomes offended, feels slighted, unappreciated, and will go to another dealership until they find someone who will listen to them.

The most positive thing we can do for our prospects is to listen to them long enough and well enough until we know what their reasons for buying are. Until they tell us what those reasons are, they do not and will not feel a part of the process. Until they tell us what those reasons for buying are, we cannot understand the prospect. Until the prospect feels understood, they will not communicate fully with us. It is a Catch-22 that simply begins with us listening, and the prospects talking.

Every prospect is just like us, they have the same wants, the same needs, the same problems, the same likes and dislikes. Every prospect we meet is crying out to be understood, and for someone to listen to them. If you are the salesperson who listens to them, and listens patiently enough for them to share with you what they really want and truly need, at a price they can afford, they will not buy from anyone but you. Because you listened to them, they will think that you are a genius.

They will feel honored to spend their money with you. And every other salesperson who ran their yapper instead of listening to the prospect, who wouldn't listen to their stories, who tried every trial close in the book on them, and hammered them to buy, that salesperson will never hear from them again. And they will send you their friends, their relatives and their neighbors. Why? Because for once in their buying life, someone shut up and listened to them.

If there is any secret to selling, it is this:

Shut your yapper. Listen to your prospects.

Chapter Eight

Don't Give Them A Business Card

This one is going to seem a little weird, but hear me out.

Don't be too quick to pass out your business card. What, do you expect them to advertise for you? They don't even know you yet.

Remember to put their self-interest first. The prospect is interested in things which benefit them. That's it. That is all of us. Most of us don't really care about helping someone else sell more. We are interested in what helps us sell more. So don't force your business card on them.

If you do a great job at letting them talk, if you ask good questions, if you listen to the answers, if you help them discover what they really want and truly need, and what they will be willing to pay for, you won't have to offer your business card. They will ask you for one.

If you are nice to them, and pay attention to them, and are honest with them, they will never forget your name. If you do your job, they will ask you for your card. Then, you can give it to them. But wait until they ask for it. If they don't ask for your card, it is because you did not do a good enough job listening to them.

The way you know if you did a really good job is when, after they have bought from you, they ask you for extra business cards.

And because they trust you, and you were willing to help them get what they really want, truly need, and in their price range, they will give you referrals, just because you listened to them.

So don't give them a business card. Wait until they ask for one.

Chapter Nine

Stop Being Enthusiastic

In the business of selling, you have heard a thousand times, "Enthusiasm sells," and, "To be enthusiastic, act enthusiastic."

Let's get real here. Not everyone is enthusiastic. Not everyone greets the day with, "I'm super, but I'll get better." Actually, if you spend any time studying the four personalities, sanguine, melancholy, choleric and phlegmatic, you'll find that *maybe* one out of four prospects *might* be enthusiastic by nature. The other 75 percent aren't enthusiastic, don't want to be, and they think there is something wrong with people who are.

I will bet that you will never have a prospect walk through your showroom door, and when you say, "How are you?" they will respond, "Super, but I'll get better." Those full of baloney lines are just that, full of baloney. Some of the lines even have a little pimiento loaf thrown in, and other kinds of slick meat you see in the deli. Normal people don't say things like that.

Your prospect does not want to be treated like some addendum to your efforts to psyche yourself up so you'll be in the mood to sell. Fake enthusiasm fools no one. Fake enthusiasm instills in most prospects a sense of danger, a quickening of their defenses, and closes the lines of genuine communication.

Now, if you are by nature enthusiastic, then be enthusiastic. But if you are not, don't fake it. Don't be a phony. People can spot it.

Just be you. Prospects would rather have a genuine salesperson than a fake one. Don't act in a way that is not you. Be real. Be genuine. When you have to act like someone you are not to get the sale, there will come a time when you will not be sure who you are. People don't like fakes.

Just be you, and allow the prospect to be themselves.

CHAPTER TEN

Stop Selling Features And Benefits

Remember that we are discussing selling from the view point of the prospect, not the salesperson.

Features and benefits do not sell cars. Prospects are not interested in features and benefits. You are. Your sales manager is. The person who designed the car is. The manufacturer is. But you are not selling to them. The prospect does not think in terms of features and benefits. Save that stuff for your sales meetings with each other.

Prospects do not buy features and benefits. The prospect will never say to you, "I would like to know about the feature of the heated steering wheel, and can you then explain how I would benefit from that feature?"

A prospect will never say to you, "Could you please do a walk around for me and tell me all you know about the features and benefits of this vehicle? I promise I will pay attention, honest I will."

Prospects do not say those things or think in those terms.

Salespeople think in those terms, but we are not selling to each other, or to the manager, or to the designer and creator of the vehicle. Features and benefits selling was invented by salespeople, for salespeople, and we think that prospects are interested in how good our presentation skills are. They are not.

Most salespeople think that they are pretty good presenters. We like to think that our demonstrations never put anyone to sleep. We like to think that we do a pretty good walk around. But it does not matter what we think. There is no commission paid on how good we think we are.

The true purpose of selling, that is, finding out what the prospect really wants and truly needs, and how much they are willing to pay for it can be accomplished without the prime time special starring us in the leading role as demonstrator par excellence.

Prospects don't buy features and benefits. They buy solutions to their problems.

If you do your selling job right, and if you ask intelligent questions, and practice patient listening, if you help the prospect discover for themselves what they really want and truly need, and how much they will pay to get the vehicle they want, you won't ever need to worry again about features and benefits.

Chapter Eleven

Stop Assuming The Close

A long time ago in seventh grade science class, Mr. Prince, my teacher wrote the word *assume* on the blackboard. He then said, and I quote, "When you assume, you make an a___ out of you and me."

And that was so long ago that he wasn't even allowed to use the word "ass." So he just underlined the word on the blackboard.

But the rule still holds true today. Everyone always tells us, "Don't assume." The reason is the same now as it was then. Assuming things makes us look bad. When we apologize we say, "I just assumed."

Everywhere we go, we are told, "Don't assume." But then in a selling situation, what do we do? We assume. We are told, "Assume the close," or, "Use the assumptive close."

> Based on national statistics, the average car shopper goes 4.2 places before they buy. So when we assume the close — we are making an ass out of ourselves three out of four times.

Why not take the advice of my seventh grade science teacher? Why don't we stop assuming the close? Why don't we stop assuming everything? The only part of the sale that we can control is our part, how we behave, what we say, what we do, how we ask questions, how we listen, how we deal with the information the prospect gives us, how honest we are, how sincere we are, and how we attempt to listen to what they really want, truly need, and are willing to pay for.

So stop assuming they are going to buy. Stop acting like they will buy with every breath they take. Don't say things like, "Well, your new car is really going to look nice in your garage," or, "When you get this baby home and drive it around, you'll feel like blah, blah, blah."

Don't assume the close. Don't assume that your selling skills are so great that no prospect can resist your powerful closes and demonstrations.

Stop assuming the close. It offends the prospect. It closes doors. It does not lead to a sincere, friendly, open selling experience for the prospect.

Chapter Twelve

That Which You May Assume

You may assume those things which are under your direct control. You may assume that it is your primary job to do your best to find out what they really want, truly need, and are willing to pay for.

You may assume that you can make plans to have an open, honest, sincere, friendly line of harmless questions, which will help the prospect discover what they want and need.

You may assume that you should talk less. If you are talking, you are not discovering what they want and need. If you are talking, you are telling them *your* story. If you are talking, you may assume that you are boring the prospect.

You may assume that you are not present in the sales process to talk.

You may assume that you are there to listen.

You may assume that your job is to ask questions. How? Well, maybe you could go down to Blockbuster and rent a Columbo tape. You could spend an evening watching the great detective in action, and learn to imitate his non-offensive, non-threatening, non-abrasive line of questioning.

Wouldn't that be better than continuing to assume everyone is going to buy? Wouldn't that be better than offending your prospects by talking too much? Wouldn't that be better than boring the prospect to death with too much product knowledge? Wouldn't your prospects respect you more and open up to you more if you just ask simple, unassuming questions?

Aren't good, sincere, no strings questions a better way to find out what the prospect really wants and needs?

Doesn't it make more sense to gently question, rather than to brashly insist on, "... here are the reasons why you should buy this car?"

Wouldn't it make for a kinder, gentler selling experience for both you and your prospect if you can control your desire to talk, to tell, to demonstrate? There is a place to do all that, but it is not until the prospect has related to you what they really want, truly need, and are willing to pay for.

After there is no doubt in your mind, or the prospect's mind, about what they really want, truly need, and are willing to pay for, then and only then are you in a secure position to help them buy.

So just plan on doing your best to find out what they want, need, and will pay for.

Chapter Thirteen

Stop Handling Objections

Selling is not talking a prospect into something they don't want, don't need and can't afford.

Selling is finding out what a prospect really wants, truly needs and is willing to pay for, then helping them get it.

If you have been selling for any length of time, you've probably heard objections. And if your sales training consisted of that old standby, "on the job training," then you probably spent a great deal of time exhibiting your vast product knowledge to most of your prospects.

Most likely, every time you really got going good, the prospect objected.

Now, they were not objecting to the product, or to the price, or to the design, or to the dealership, they were objecting to *you*. They were objecting to the way you were rushing them through the sales process; they were objecting to your high pressure tactics. The truth is, they just did not like the way they were being treated.

And when they objected, you handled the objection, and then started your vast array of presentational skills again, and just when you really got rolling, they objected again. And of course you handled the objection again, and again and again. And the more you handled, the more they objected.

And so you watched a sales video, and one of the instructors said, "Close on every objection." Now that is really a classic in the old school of selling back when Noah was building the ark. "Close on every objection."

Hmmmmm, let me see if I have this right? The prospect is going to object. And when the prospect objects, I am supposed to try to close the sale, just after the prospect tells me why they don't want to buy. Wow, why didn't I think of that?

Note to self: If I am getting objections, there is something wrong with my behavior, my attitude, my delivery, or all three.

If your sincere desire is to find out what they really want, what they truly need, and what price they are willing to pay, YOU WILL NOT GET OBJECTIONS.

Objections are a sign that you are doing something wrong. You are pushing the prospect too fast, pressuring too much, trying too hard, not listening enough, or just mishandling the prospect. They do not like it, so they object. But please know that they are not objecting to your product. They are objecting to you.

And until you accept personal responsibility for getting objections, you will continue to get objections.

Remember that the purpose of selling is to help the prospect discover what they really want, truly need, and what they are willing to pay for. If you do that gently, sincerely, and in the best interest of the prospect, it is not necessary to get objections. Why would any prospect object, when they were allowed to discuss what they want, need, and would pay for, especially if the salesperson then took them to look at what they said they wanted, and were willing to pay for? What is there for them to object to? Nothing. Period. End of story.

If you would like to stop getting objections, here is the process. It is not rocket science. There are only three basic steps to the process of avoiding objections:

1. Realize why you get objections. You get them because you are rushing the prospect, because you are not listening to the prospect, because you are forcing your needs and wants on them, and you are hoping to talk them into buying something which you want to sell, more than they want to buy. It won't work.

2. Learn to ask questions. Go to Blockbuster and rent or buy a Columbo tape. Watch and learn from the master of questions. Practice asking harmless, non-offensive questions. Find out

what your prospect really wants. You cannot find out if you are running your yapper. You can't find out what the prospect wants if you are doing your features and benefits thing. You can only find out what they want, need and will pay for by asking questions and listening to the answer.

3. Learn to listen to the answers. Most salespeople interrupt, ignore, answer their own questions, and just don't listen to the prospect. To ask a question of the prospect and then to answer it, or to not listen to their answer is worse than not asking the question.

Note to self:

1. **Objections are my fault**
2. **I must learn to ask questions**
3. **I must learn to listen to the answers**

This is not fourth year calculus. It is so simple that most salespeople miss it. Look, if we just help the prospect discover what they really want and truly need, and if we go one step further and ask them what they are really willing to pay to get what they want, and then if we are smart enough to get them what they want, at the price they want to pay,

How hard is that?

What we need to overcome is the habit of trying to control the sale, trying to control the customer, trying to qualify to the point that we think we are their financial guru, in short, we need to break the habit of trying to run the show.

The nano-second that we realize that we do not run the show, we will start selling more cars, making more money, and we will be able to help more people get what they want.

Chapter Fourteen

Stop Educating The Prospect

This chapter is going to stick in your craw a bit. This one will be hard for you to do. It shouldn't be, but it will. Matter of fact, your manager will probably go nuts when they hear you do this. But, if you want to sell more and make more and help more prospects get what they want, you have no choice but to master this one.

Stop educating the prospect. You are not a school house. You are not a college. You are not a teacher. You are not a professor. Your presentations are not supposed to be dazzling displays of your vast knowledge about your product. (Listen up, all you retired teachers who are now in the real world and selling for a living.)

The age old rule is: Sell today, educate tomorrow.

Does your manager pay you a commission for your demo's? How much extra do you make when you put a prospect to sleep with your product knowledge? If your place is like our place, the answer is: zip, zero, nada.

You don't get paid for showing how smart you are.

The prospect does not care what you know. What the prospect cares about is whether or not your product will meet their wants, needs, and budget. The limits and boundaries of your part of the selling process are always set by the prospect. (If you are doing your job.)

"What does my prospect want to know?" That is the only question you need to concern yourself with. This whole selling thing is not about you. It is about them, your prospect, what they want, what they need, what they will pay for.

And the whole truth of the matter is *that they will only be willing to pay for what they really want and truly need.*

> Anything you do or say in the selling process which does not focus directly on wants, needs and budget is harmful to the sales process, and reveals a lack of sincerity for the prospect.

You are not in sales to do the proverbial dog and pony show. If you are not showing them the vehicle they really want, it does not matter how great your presentation is.

If you are showing them something which they cannot afford, it does not matter how good a job you do, that presentation will always get a no.

Stop educating the prospect. It does not help you get a sale.

When you educate the prospect, it gives your prospect information so the next place they go, they can make a better buying decision. Think about this scenario: the average car buyer goes 4.2 places before they buy a car. If the first three salespeople do the proverbial dog and pony show, by the time the prospect gets to the fourth salesperson, the prospect knows more about the vehicle than this salesperson. Three other salespeople have educated the prospect for free. And for that, they received no commission, just the practice.

Let the prospect educate you. Let them be the teacher. You be the student. They are there to tell you what they want, what they need, what they will pay for, and the why to all of these things. All you have to do is listen, take notes, and then get them what they want.

So stop educating the prospect. Educating the prospect is for next week when you follow up the sale. Educating the prospect is for after they get what they want and need. Then you call them and say, "Oh by the way, there are some things about your car I didn't get a chance to go over with you. Do you want to stop back in, or should I come to your place?"

Stop educating the prospect. Let them educate you. The commission is much greater this way.

CHAPTER FIFTEEN

Stop Making Excuses

One of the biggest obstacles in the way of sales success is excuse making.

What is an excuse? An excuse is a reason, and it could be a good one, for not doing what we were supposed to do.

Using an excuse is when we blame someone or something for not doing what we were supposed to do.

Any excuse we use becomes self-perpetuating and self-defeating. As long as we are willing to blame someone else, or some thing else, we never have to change. Because in our eyes, it is not our fault. It's his fault, it's her fault, it's their fault.

As long as we blame someone else, we will never see the need to change.

Here are some excuses which will keep us from succeeding:

It's my wife's fault
It's my husband's fault
It's the kids' fault
It's the economy
It's 9-11
It's the republicans
It's the democrats
It's the independents
I'm too fat
I'm too thin
I'm too young
I'm too old
I don't have enough education
I'm over-qualified
My skills aren't good enough yet
I'm too tired
I'm too energetic
I'm scared
I'm not feeling well
I'm black

I'm white
I'm brown
I'm Asian
I'm a woman
I'm a man
I was told I would never amount to anything
It's my parents' fault
It's the neighborhood
It's my friends
It's the school I attended
I don't have any money
My parents were rich
It's too hot
It's too cold
It's raining
It's snowing
It's too windy
It's too late
It's too early
It's my manager
It's our sales literature
It's GM
It's Ford

It's Chrysler
It's Saturn
It's blah, blah, blah

Do you get the idea? **As long as we are willing to blame some one, some thing, or some condition, we don't have to change.**

As long as we feel that we don't need to change, because the way things are now is someone else's fault, we will not change. And if we do not change, nothing in our lives will ever get any better. Family relationships, work relationships, money relationships, our circle of friends, our careers, as long as we do not see the need to change, our lives are doomed to mediocrity forever.

STOP MAKING EXCUSES.

A man once went to his neighbor to borrow his lawnmower. The neighbor said no. The man asked, "Why can't I borrow your lawnmower?"

Neighbor said, "I'm making soup."

Man said, "What does making soup have to do with me borrowing your lawnmower?'

"Nothing," said the neighbor, "but if I don't want you to borrow my lawnmower, any excuse will do."

Any excuse, even if it is your favorite, will keep you from success in sales. If you plan on succeeding in sales, just make up your mind to earn everything you get. Don't expect much help. Don't complain when it seems that no one wants you to do much better than them. Don't blame the manager, the weather, the economy, or the products, just make up your mind that your success depends just about entirely on what you do, what you decide to do next, and your own acceptance of personal responsibility.

Note to self: If I expect any progress in my selling career, I need to accept personal responsibility for where I am in my career, how much I am making, and where I want to go in the future.

Chapter Sixteen

Acceptance Of Personal Responsibility

The opposite of making excuses is the acceptance of personal responsibility.

If you want to change things in your life, in your sales career, and in your present financial condition, the key is to accept full and immediate responsibility for where you are, how you got there, how much you make, how much you want to make, and where you want to go in life.

And to do that, you must stop blaming people or circumstances for why you are where you are. A little secret: until we are willing to accept full and final responsibility for ourselves, we will never rise above where we are now, we will never make any more money than we are making now, and we will never break the cycle we are in now.

Immediate acceptance of personal responsibility means that we break with the past, and stop blaming others.

It is all mental, and it is not rocket science. All you need to do is realize that where you are is your responsibility, and where you want to go is your responsibility.

So, here is your fresh start:

As of this date, ___/___/___, I, ______________, will no longer blame my_________________, my________________, my________________, or my_____________, for who I am, what I have, and where I want to go. I am responsible for myself, my life and my career. I will do what is necessary to change. I will set goals, and if they are to be accomplished, it is my responsibility to do so. God helping me, today I accept full responsibility for myself, my life and my career.

Signed ______________________________

Chapter Seventeen

Don't Overdress

Dress for success is out. Everyone knows about it by now. The power pants, the expensive silk ties, the dark colors meant to impress and intimidate, that stuff may work on television, but real life is not much like television. There are no cue cards and laugh tracks.

Casual is in. Business casual is in.

Don't dress for success; dress for your customers.

If you live in a rural community, dress like your customers.

If you live in a banking community, dress like your customers.

If you live in suburbia, dress like your customers.

If you live next to Land's End, you really have it made.

It's pretty simple. If you overdress, you are putting a barrier between you and your prospects. You are placing an obstacle between you and them.

People buy from people they like. People buy from people they are comfortable with. If by over-dressing, you make people uncomfortable with you, you will have to work twice as hard to get the sale, if you get it at all.

If the prospect sees your white shirt embossed with your initials, your silk ties, your gold Rolex, your silk suit or sport coat, if they are not dressed the same way, they will not feel comfortable.

If you want to sell more, you need more prospects who are comfortable with you.

If the way you dress is getting in the way, change what you wear. It may not be a big deal to us, but it is to the prospect. Anything that makes the prospect feel more comfortable during the selling process is a big deal to them, and therefore to us.

As salespeople, we need to be in the business of taking down barriers to understanding, not putting them up because of a false impression we have of ourselves.

Dress for your prospects.

www.landsend.com

Chapter Eighteen

Stop Telling Your Prospects Why They Should Buy

If you are still in the habit of talking too much, instead of listening to the prospect, then you will find yourself telling them why they should buy what you want to sell them.

What you want to sell them, for your reasons, based on what you think they need, does not compute with them as valid reasons why they should buy.

It might make perfect sense to you, but then, who cares? The prospect does not. You won't be driving the vehicle. The prospect will. You won't be paying for the vehicle. The prospect will. You won't be taking care of the vehicle for the next three, four or five years. The prospect will.

> The majority of prospects do not buy from you because you are telling them what they need to do.

Unless people where you are, are a lot different than the people where I am, people don't like someone else telling them what to do. They like to make their own decisions. But if we are too busy running our yapper to listen to them, we don't give them a chance to make their decision. Amateur salespeople try to make the decision for them. Professional salespeople let the prospect make the decision.

Many selling situations come down to a power struggle. If the selling situation becomes a tug of war, the salesperson is usually going to lose. If you are playing tug of war, and trying too hard, then you are probably telling them what to do, what to buy, instead of them telling you what they want to buy and why.

Stop telling them. Helloo-o-o-o — they don't care what you think. They don't care how you feel. They don't care about how good you think you are. All they care about is how they think, how they feel, and what they want. Really. They are the customer. They are always right. Remember, they have already justified in their minds what they want, why they want and need it, and how much they can afford to spend to get it. Don't let a run-away yapper get in the way of finding out what they really want, truly need, and are willing to pay for.

Stop telling them. They did not pull on your lot or walk into your showroom so you could tell them things. They came in so they could tell you what they want. Hello-o-o-o — let them tell you. Close the yapper.

Listen, listen and listen some more.

When you're telling, you're not selling.

Chapter Nineteen

Start Letting Your Prospects Tell You What They Want To Buy

Blockbuster store, get a Columbo tape, learn to ask unassuming questions.

Just do it.

The key to selling more cars and making more money is: listening to your prospects. Here's why: no one listens to them. The wife doesn't pay attention to the husband. The husband doesn't pay attention to the wife. The kids have tuned them both out. People at work don't listen to them or respect them.

And then you come along and ignore what they want, you tell them what they should have, based on your reasons, and they are thinking, "I can get this treatment at home." And they go somewhere else.

Every prospect who drives on your lot, or walks in your showroom is terribly under-listened to. If you just listen to them, pay attention to them, let them tell their story, let them ramble on about what they did during the war, how they met, how they decided to buy a new car, why they decided to buy a new car, whatever. Just pay attention to them.

If you pay attention, if you just listen, if you are sincere, you will be the first person in months who really listened to them. Funny thing is, they will think that you are a genius. And all you did was listen and ask a few questions.

If you want to double your sales, then double the time you listen to your prospects.

If you want to triple your sales, then triple the time you spend paying attention to your prospects. It really is almost that simple.

Chapter Twenty

Take Notes On What The Prospect Tells You

Columbo questions; harmless, unassuming questions, and take notes while they are talking.

One of the most powerful psychological tools available to salespeople is the ability to pay attention, really pay attention; to listen, to really listen; and then to take notes in the process.

When is the last time you were talking to someone, and they thought that what you had to say was so important that they took notes?

Most prospects are terribly under-listened to. No one, no one, takes notes on what they say. You want to distance yourself from your competition? Take notes on what they say. If you do, you will be their hero forever.

People like people who pay attention to them. And there is nothing that says, "I am paying attention to you," like writing down what they tell you. Try it with your wife or husband. Try it with your kids. Taking notes shows that you want to know and remember what they are saying to you.

Now, don't be diaphanous. Don't just write down their name, address, telephone number, and how much they will pay.

Write down important things, the reasons they want to buy, what they like, what they don't like, how soon they need it, why they want it, what will happen if they don't get it, how many other places have they shopped, just write down most everything they are willing to tell you. If you fill three or four notepads with real information on real prospects with real needs, you can live on the referral business.

The secret to getting referrals is to make the person in front of you feel important. Not getting referrals is not the problem. It is just a symptom. When we are not getting referrals, it is because we are not treating our present prospects like they want to be treated.

If they do not like the way they are being treated, why should they give us any referrals? They shouldn't. And they won't.

If you treat them well, pay attention to them, take notes on what they tell you, if you help them discover what they really want, truly need and are willing to pay for, THEY WILL OFFER REFERRALS.

Note to self: I need to start taking notes.

Chapter Twenty-one

Stop Qualifying The Prospect

I know, your manager says to Meet & Greet, Qualify, Present and Close, that's the way we've always done it here and that's the way we're going to keep doing it, I'm in charge and blah, blah, blah. Okay, that's great, can we move along?

Stop qualifying the prospect. Who do you think you are, the IRS? Their banker? Their accountant? Their financial confidant?

Don't use stupid pet tricks to try to find out how much money they have. You know, what neighborhood they live in, try to get their telephone prefix and then hope for an influential part of town. Don't play games with them. They know the games, and when they find out you are playing games with them, you will offend them and they will never buy from you.

Your first job is to listen to them, to let them tell you what they really want, truly need, and how much they are willing to pay. The other information will come out. They will tell you. But it is your job to get all the other information first. Why do they want it? Why do they need it?

How many other places have they been? Why didn't they buy at one of those places? What made them come to your lot?

If you ask the right questions, and wait patiently and sincerely for the answers, all the other information will come out at the right time. If you push too hard for the qualifying information too early, the prospect is offended, feels like a number, feels cheap, feels used, and why should they put up with that treatment?

So, stop with the cute qualifying questions. If you do your real job, which is to listen, learn, discover, be sincere, be patient, they will give you more qualifying information than you want or need.

Too difficult? Have we talked about going to the Blockbuster store and getting a Columbo tape? You know, Lt. Columbo, the unassuming detective who appears to stumble around, asking a lot of harmless questions. But, he always gets his information.

> The harder you try for qualifying information before you get the trust and respect of the prospect, the less information you will get, and the less reliable the information will be.

Chapter Twenty-two

Get A Timex

If you think much about human relations, and you probably should, there is one rule which stands out above the others:

You should always let the prospect feel more okay than you do.

What does that mean? Well, first it means that you stop trying to impress the prospect with your appearance, your speech, the words you use, the things you do.

Contrived, controlled, dress for success appearances always make the prospect feel a bit uncomfortable. The exception here is if you are dealing only with dress for success, rich, elegant, Rolex wearing, gold jewelry dangling prospects. But if the majority of your prospects are not in that weight class, then this chapter is for you.

Get a Timex. Stop with the Rolex. Stop trying to impress prospects with how much money you may be making. The prospect does not care about buying from the number one salesperson in the country. That is only a fig newton in your imagination. Remember, the prospect has more reasons to buy than we do to sell. The prospect has an idea of what they want, what they need and how much they will spend.

When you smack them between the eyes with your gold Rolex, your cloud of Brut, your gold bracelet on the other wrist, the gold chain around your neck, and your pinky ring on your cute little finger, they forget all about what they came in for, and they notice you. And they ask themselves if they should be handing you their money, because you obviously don't need it. There is no commission when they notice how cool you are. You might get your ego stroked, but that doesn't get much commission either.

So stop trying to impress your prospects. You can make enough to earn a Rolex, just don't wear it in front of your prospects. Don't confuse what you wear with the reasons the prospect buys. A nice, expensive, gold, special order Rolex never sold a car, but a Rolex and a pompous attitude have certainly cost many a sale.

The number one rule in human relations is:

Always let the prospect feel more okay than you do.

If you are going to observe that rule, then make sure you dress, talk, and act like the people who are about to hand you a big stack of their money.

Save the Rolex and pinky rings to impress other salespeople. Too much gold and silk makes the prospect uncomfortable.

Uncomfortable prospects keep shopping until they find a salesperson they can be comfortable with.

Stop with the Rolex already.

Chapter Twenty-three

Don't Take All Their Money

Don't take all their money. The operative word here is "their." It is not our money. It is their money. And if you want to sell more cars, make more money and help more people get what they want, then you have to stop taking all their money.

Here's a new rule: leave some money on the table.

When a prospect tells you that they can afford a payment of four hundred dollars a month, they have shared with you some very important, very personal information. Sacred information, if you will.

And if that is their honest interpretation of their financial situation, it is well nigh blasphemous to send them home with a payment of $441.99.

If that sort of a bump is not a self-centered move on the part of the salesperson, I don't know what to call it.

A fair profit is necessary, right, and must be included in the sale. No one can stay in business if they do not make a fair profit. But don't take all the prospect's money. It is not fair, it is not right, and in the long run it will cost much more than you will be paid.

> When prospects finally trust you enough to tell you what they really want, what they truly need, and how much they are willing to pay to get it, you are at that point entering into a fiduciary relationship with that prospect. That means that you are in a position of trust. What you do with that trust is very important, and is a clear definition of what kind of person you really are.

If you sell them what they really want, and truly need, and in the price range they told you they can afford, you will get all their business, and you will have more referrals than you can handle.

Not getting referrals is not a problem. It is a symptom. The real problem is that you didn't earn enough trust, that you didn't treat the prospect the way they want to be treated, so they were not comfortable sharing their friends and family with you. Not getting referrals is a sign that your prospects don't trust you.

But if you don't take all their money, and they get what they really want and truly need, at the price they wanted to spend, or less, they will tell everyone they know about you, they will pass out your cards, and they will send you referrals.

And all because you let them decide how much they were willing to spend.

When your prospect, under pressure, spends more than they want to, and when you push them to do it, they think of you once a month, and those thoughts are not favorable.

In junior high school we were all taught the Latin phrase, Caveat Emptor, let the buyer beware. And in the back of our minds, we think that is the rule.

In professional selling, that is not the rule. The rule for professional salespeople is: *Let the seller beware.* The seller must beware of greed, and shortcuts, and abrasive techniques, and misusing the prospect, but above all, the seller must beware of taking too much money. That is why the discovery process of finding out how much the prospect has budgeted for this purchase is so important.

Find out what their budget is, then stay within that budget, or below it.

The seller must beware of getting only one sale, when the referrals and repeat business for hundreds of people are riding on every sale. Professional selling means treating each prospect respectfully and carefully when it comes to money.

If you want more repeat business, and more referrals, leave some money on the table.

**By the way,
When you force the prospect,
When you hammer them,
When you trial close them,
When you ignore their wishes,
When you tell them what
<u>You think they need,</u>
When you bump them,
When you switch them,
When you trick them,**

**You are killing the goose
that lays the golden eggs.**

Chapter Twenty-four

Prepare For The Prospect, Not For The Sales Call

The more you prepare for a sales call, the less likely you are to sell something. Here's why:

Many salespeople study product knowledge, features and benefits, pricing structure, sales literature, what to say, how to say it, when to say it, who to say it to, how to handle objections, and yada, yada, yada, all in preparation for dealing with a live prospect.

So you already know what is going to happen when an unsuspecting, unassuming, unsophisticated prospect walks in the door. That's right, the well educated, well prepared salesperson is going to show the prospect how well prepared, how smart, how great a salesperson he really is. Yak, yak, yak, no sale.

Don't prepare for the sales call; prepare for the prospect. Prepare yourself to listen and ask questions.

> Ask the prospect about their special wants and needs. Let them tell you why they should buy. It is what *they* know that will determine whether or not you get a sale. They are the focal point. Learn from them. If you listen to them, they will enjoy telling you, and as you listen and take notes on what they say, they will respect you. They will even trust you. People buy from people they trust.

Prospects do not buy from the smartest, best dressed, loudest, pushiest salesperson. Prospects buy from people they trust. If you are going to prepare for sales calls, then prepare <u>yourself</u> to listen and learn. Prepare to ask questions. Prepare to take notes. Prepare to find out everything you can about why the prospect is going to buy. Prepare to find out what they really want, truly need, and how much they are willing to pay to get it.

That is the only preparation which will equip you to help the prospect, and get paid for doing it. Imagine that, getting paid to help someone get what they want. How simple is that?

Chapter Twenty-five

Don't Tell The Prospect Everything You Know

Product knowledge is a dangerous thing.

Sales technique is more dangerous.

They are both dangerous because there is the tendency to use them at the wrong time, and in the wrong way.

Since you are this far into the book and still reading, may I make several points? Thank you.

You should know everything there is to know about your product.

You should be the best presenter in your dealership.

You should study and know the absolute best sales technique In the world today.

You should be able to execute that technique flawlessly.

The danger is in using the product knowledge and sales technique at the wrong time, and in the wrong place in the sales process. For now, just remember this: Don't tell everything you know. If you do, you'll tell too much, the prospect won't listen, and the prospect won't buy.

> Let the prospect tell you everything they know. That's why they came to see you. They did not come in so you could sell them a car. They came in because they need a vehicle, and they want to tell you about it. They want it. You have it. Let them talk you into helping them get what they want.

Don't tell them everything you know.

Chapter Twenty-six

Don't Get Commission Breath

Prospects have more reasons to buy than we do to sell.

We have one reason to sell. We need the money. But if we need the money too much, it shows to the prospect. They will sense it. The prospect can always smell commission breath.

Commission breath is defined this way: when you need a sale so bad, the prospect can smell it on your breath.

It's pretty simple, but commission breath can lose many a sale. When we need a sale so bad *the prospect* can smell it, the prospect will not buy. And if we begin to try harder, pushing more, pressuring more, trying more sales tricks, more closes, more product knowledge, the more the prospect will resist.

There is a cure for commission breath: Relax. Stop pushing so hard. Stop selling. Stop trying to sell. Just go out and see people and find out what they want, need, and are willing to pay for. Then help them get it.

If you are having trouble selling, you may have sales halitosis, commission breath. You can get over it by not trying so hard. Let the prospect have buying breath. Let them tell you why, when, where, how and how much. It's okay if they have buying breath. Don't interrupt them when they are telling you what they want, why they need it, and how much they will pay to get it. Listen, ask questions, take notes.

CHAPTER TWENTY-SEVEN

Stop Talking So Much

This page is pretty simple.

This page is pretty straight to the point.

The number one complaint in America about salespeople is that they talk too much.

If you want to help more people get what they want, sell more and make more money, *stop talking so much.* Talking too much will cost you a fortune in your sales lifetime.

You know the old line, two ears, one mouth, listen twice as much as you talk. It is true. No one likes someone who talks all the time.

The number one complaint in America about salespeople is that they talk too much.

When you talk too much, the prospect can't get a word in. They can't tell you what they really want, how bad they want it, what they are going to do with it, how much they need it, how long they've wanted it, and how much they will pay for it, and how they are going to pay for it.

The number one complaint in America about salespeople is that they talk too much.

When you are talking, it means that your prospect cannot talk. That is bad. Okay? Stop talking so much. Remember, the prospect probably just came from another salesperson who would not listen to them. The prospect has been driving from dealership to dealership, and not one salesperson has listened to him.

Hey, stop talking so much. Let the prospect talk. You never get paid based on what you say. Your commission check is based entirely on what the prospect says. Be quiet and let them say it already.

The number one complaint in America about salespeople is that they talk too much.

CHAPTER TWENTY-EIGHT

Don't Have A Vanity Wall

Think for a minute to the last time you were in your attorney's office. Remember all the super-impressive things hanging on the wall? That is called a vanity wall. It is usually directly behind the attorney, so the poor victim in the chair facing the attorney can't miss seeing and reading it. For your first time in his/her office, your attorney usually leaves the room to "look for a file." And you thought that they really needed to go look for a file. Yeah, right. As if they don't have people who can pull files for them. They are leaving the room to give to you time to be impressed with all the certificates on the wall.

The sheepskins are there, the summa cum whatevers, the awards, the clubs, the pictures, all meant to impress the heck out of you. Most of us are not impressed. Actually we are put off. All those wall hangings make us feel belittled, intimidated and depressed. And we think that we're about to pay for some of those college bills, and we didn't come in to do that. We came in because we had a problem.

Class, are we getting the idea? Get rid of the plaques which say, "Salesperson of the Month." Get rid of those certificates which say, "Number one Salesperson." Get rid of the trophies, the ribbons and the sales awards. Those things make the prospect feel belittled, intimidated and depressed. And no matter how proud you are of your awards, you will never get the prospect to feel that way.

> Prospects who feel belittled, intimidated and depressed do not buy. Period. Those prospects go to your competition. Remember this: every award you hang on your wall behind your desk is going to send a prospect a week to your competition. You went to public school. You do the math.

If your awards and plaques make you feel better about yourself, then put them at home, above the bathroom mirror, where you can see them and do the little Jack Horner thing. But at work, get rid of everything that makes your prospect think about you; get rid of everything that makes the prospect feel like finding another salesperson who isn't bragging about how great they think they are.

Your plaques and awards are causing your prospects to find another salesperson who isn't good enough yet to get plaques and awards. They feel deep down that the amateur will get them a better deal. Your prospect feels good when they are around salespeople who have not won a lot of awards. It makes them feel better about themselves. And prospects who feel good about themselves buy from salespeople who make them feel that way.

It doesn't matter if you are the greatest the world has ever seen, you don't want your prospects to know that you are the best, the brightest and the highest paid. You want them to think that they are smarter than you, brighter than you, and making more money than you.

Look, it's all about the money. Prospects like to buy from salespeople they can feel superior to.

So let them feel superior. Let them buy. Let them feel good about buying.

Tell your boss thanks for the plaques, the awards, the ribbons, the diamond tie tacks and the ad in the newspaper that says, "Salesperson Of the Month." Thank your boss for those things, but don't put them anywhere near where your prospects can see them.

Remember Blockbuster? The Columbo tape? Mr. Unassuming? Mr/Mrs/Ms Master of questioning? If you haven't gone to rent or buy the tape yet, you got some 'splainin' to do.

If you hide all your plaques, awards and etcetera, and if you humble yourself to let your prospects feel superior to you, you will sell enough and make enough money that someday, you will loan your attorney money. No joke.

Chapter Twenty-nine

Halftime

Tell you what. You're about half-way through the book.

Some of the book is probably getting Boring and Repetitious.

But, take heart. While you are learning what not to do, your competition is busy doing what you are learning not to do.

That means that they are sending prospects to you. Can you say, "Ka-ching?"

All you need to do is treat the prospects exactly the opposite of what your competition is doing.

So take heart. It is what you are learning NOT to do, that will set you apart from the rest of the salespeople out there.

You're different. Congratulations!!!

Chapter Thirty

Author's Apology

You know, in looking at most of these chapter titles, most of them are written in the form of a negative: don't do this, stop doing that, get rid of this; and that is for a reason.

> It is because most of our selling brings a negative response from our prospects.

And in order to be positive, and to write a book that will bring a positive response from your prospect, many of these issues must be addressed from what seems to be a negative viewpoint.

There is just no positive way to tell a salesperson: You talk too much. Shut up and listen to your prospect.

But if you, by not doing these things that we are talking about, increase your sales and profits, and make a positive difference in your prospect's lives and in your bank account, then by all accounts, every chapter title is nothing but positive.

Positive is when you make more money. Positive is when you help more prospects get what they want. Positive is when your prospects trust you so much that they offer you names and send you referrals. Positive is when you have more money than month.

So stop not letting them buy. Stop not letting them talk. Let them talk and talk and buy and buy. And when you do that, you will think that this is the most positive book on selling that you have ever read.

Be positive. Stop doing negative things.

Chapter Thirty-one

There Are No Unreasonable Prospects

Prospects have reasons for everything. There are prospects who will work you, test you, try you, use you, abuse you, but that is because they are prospects. They are your prospects, and they have a right to their reasons. You may not agree with their reasons, but you must let them know that you think that they have a right to those reasons.

There are no unreasonable prospects. There are prospects with reasons, and many times when they try to express those reasons to the salesperson, the salesperson will not listen, will not pay attention, and dismisses the prospect as unreasonable.

Big mistake.

In the prospect's mind, that salesperson is unreasonable, and the prospect will tell anyone who will listen to make sure they avoid that salesperson. You do the math.

Your greatest, best and most loyal prospect is the one who at first seems to you to be unreasonable.

Your best prospect is the one who rant and raves, who complains about the economy, the prices, the manufacturer. Why do you think they do that? They are looking for a salesperson who does not get emotionally involved. If you get mad, get aggravated, and try to get even, you lose. And you will be to the prospect just like the other salespeople that he tried to work.

> If you just listen, and seek to understand, and put yourself in their shoes, eventually they will simmer down, and then you can find out what the real problem is, and work from a position of understanding.

But there is no such thing as an unreasonable prospect. There are prospects who like to rant and rave and brag and intimidate and push others around. They don't have many friends. If you put up with them, they can rant and rave themselves into buying. Let them buy.

Chapter Thirty-two

Stopwiththefasttalk

Now it could be that neurolinguisticly speaking, you are a visual person and you normally talk fast.

It could be that according to Hippocrates' study of the humors, you may be a sanguine and you just enjoy talking fast and loud.

It's your nature. It's your habit. It's what you do. You talk fast.

That is nice, but it won't help you in selling.

Prospects don't like fast talkers. Men don't like fast talkers. Women certainly don't like fast talking salesmen. And since 99 percent of your sales are going to be to men or women, it might be wise to slow down your speech patterns.

When a prospect hears a salesperson talking fast, they think that the salesperson has something to hide, something to sneak through, and the prospect begins to lose trust in the salesperson.

Whether or not this assessment by the prospect is accurate is not the question. It is the perception of the prospect, and we all know that to the prospect, perception is reality. The end result is that the prospect does not feel confident buying from a fast talker. So, they don't buy.

How much commission is there when they don't buy?

Even if your parents talk fast, if you were taught to talk fast in high school and college, and even if you won awards in speech class for being the fastest talker, it does not matter.

You must talk slow enough and deliberate enough so that the prospect trusts you, understands you and comprehends everything you say. Listen to your prospects. Three out of four of them talk slowly and deliberately. Do the same for them.

Stop talking fast. More prospects will trust you, more prospects will buy from you, and you will sell more and make more.

Chapter Thirty-three

You Cannot Talk Anyone Into Anything

I have some old books on selling. One of them has a tattered and torn cover, and the price on this full size hardback book is $3.75. That should tell you how old the book is. The cover of the book is priceless.

Priceless, that is, if you learn to do the opposite of what the book teaches.

The cover of the book shows a man, the salesman, standing over the end of the desk, pounding one fist on the desk, while holding the order form in his other hand. The prospect, meanwhile, cowers in his chair, apparently mesmerized by the enthusiasm of the towering bully of a salesman.

If a picture is worth a thousand words, this one is worth a fortune in commissions, if you never do it like this.

A man convinced against his will is of the same opinion still.

Don't yell. Don't argue. Don't try to convince. You cannot talk anyone into anything. Period. You've probably tried it with your spouse, or your kids. How did it work? Were you happy with the end result? Probably not, because it usually does not work. All of us who have a spouse and children know that it does not work. You cannot talk people into anything they do not want to do. Oh, it might work sometimes, in the short run for little things. But in the long run, with important things, it simply does not work. It doesn't work because we all have wills and emotions and desires.

We all have our own reasons for wanting to do things our way. And in this instance, families are not all that different from the business of selling. When a person or prospect has a reason that is valid to him/her about doing something or not doing something, all the money, candy, chocolate and flowers in the world will not budge them. It is a foundational principle of human nature — *you cannot talk anyone into anything that they do not want to do.*

Yet we get into sales and we think that our job is to talk people into things. Let's wise up. You may as well try to reverse the law of gravity as to try to talk someone into something they do not want to do. So how's about we stop trying to talk others into doing what we think they should do.

They won't.

How's about we stop trying to get others to see things our way?

They can't.

An easier way is to try to figure out what they want, what they need, how bad they want and need it, and then try to help them get it.

And that, friends, is a whole lot easier than forcing them to decide, making them choose, pushing them to a close, shoving them over the edge, and trial closing them to death.

Prospects cannot see things our way. So let's stop trying to force them to see things our way.

Here's a novel idea: How about we try to see things their way?

If you try this, the prospect is liable to faint. You will hear things like, "You are actually listening to me?" "You actually understand what I mean?"

Now when they tell you that, because you learned to shut up and listen, you can send a bonus check to the address in the back of this book, or you can just put the extra commission in your bank account. But they will tell you that, IF you try to see things their way, try to figure out what they want, and then help them get it.

Chapter Thirty-four

Marriage And Family Break

In teaching classes and holding seminars, I always try to get participants to practice these principles. And the easiest place to practice these principles is at home, with the spouse and children.

I have this theory that if a salesperson is having trouble listening to his/her prospects at work, that salesperson is probably having the same trouble listening to his/her spouse at home. Ditto for the kids.

If a salesperson is having trouble trying to talk his prospects into seeing things his way, it is a pretty safe bet that the same salesperson is forcing his ideas on his wife and kids. And of course that leads to the same rejection at home that it does at work.

So, if you are looking for the perfect training ground to practice these things, start listening to your husband/wife/children. Seek to understand them. Listen to them. Find out what they really want. Find out what they truly need. Then help them get it.

Sales training begins at home.

The day you start trying to understand your spouse and children is the day that you will begin to listen better to prospects. And when you learn to do that, you will sell more, make more and help more people get what they want.

These principles will work at home, with your wife, your husband and with your children.

Chapter Thirty-five

Never Beat Up The Competition

Always talk nice about your competition. This will surprise your boss, and amaze the competition. You can never impress a prospect by running down the place they just came from, or the place they may go next.

Matter of fact, the worse things you say about the competition, the quicker your prospect will go over there to see if what you said is true.

Talk nice about your competition. Let your customers go over to the competitor's lot to see their cars. Don't be afraid of that. Your prospects are adults; they'll go anyway.

The strongest selling point in that situation is that you must be nicer to deal with, more understanding, you must listen more, you must work harder to find out what they want, need and are willing to pay for. Once you do those things and the prospect trusts you, if they go ten more places, they will always come back to you.

All you did was listen, understand and help them. Funny thing, that is exactly what they wanted.

Talk nice about the competition.

I am waiting patiently for a dealership to use the following advertisement in the newspaper, on the radio, or on television:

To all our customers: If our salespeople do not listen to what you want, to what you need, in the price range you are willing to spend, I will personally drive you to any of our competing dealers.

Signed............the owner

Chapter Thirty-six

Don't Use The Impending Event Technique

The impending event technique is when a salesperson says something like, "The price goes up on Friday." The pressure in this case is upon the prospect, from the salesperson, to buy today, because of something that the dealership may do, on purpose, against the interests of the prospect.

That's a great idea; why didn't I think of that? Let's just try to scare them into buying today. I'll bet that one really works. Ever tried to scare someone into doing something? How did it work?

So don't use the impending event technique. Why? Because everyone else is doing the same thing. Everyone else is telling your prospect, "You gotta buy today," "you gotta buy today."

Remember foundational concept number one? Prospects have more reasons to buy than we do to sell? Here's another concept about like that one:

Prospects have their own time schedule and their own impending events. All you need to do is find out what their impending events are.

If the prospect is on the way to a family reunion, and wants to go in style and impress the family, that is for them an impending event. That is for them an ultimate event. It is not contrived by the dealership or by the salesperson. No special deal, no great sale, no "this week only" sale will ever place the pressure on that prospect like the pressure the prospect has already placed on himself.

Hint, hint, hint: all you need to do is find out from them, what their impending event is, and then your job becomes helping them get what they want to relieve the pressure they have placed on themselves.

(How easy is that?)

Chapter Thirty-seven

Go For Win/Win

Win/lose is no good. When you win and they lose, you are costing yourself and your dealership a fortune in future business lost. Win/lose is when you win and they lose. Win/lose is the antecedent to one of the biggest problems facing salespeople in the car business today: "What do I do with the prospect who is upside down?"

Answer: there is nothing you can do, except to make sure that you don't do the same to any of your prospects. A prospect who is upside down, is upside down because someone played win/lose.

The real definition of win/lose is: lose/lose. When a salesperson takes advantage of a prospect, both parties lose.

A buyer who gets hosed is an upside down buyer the next time, and they will never be back, and neither will their friends and family ever be back.

David Thomas, the Lexus Guy from Dallas, says that every prospect knows 200 people. You do the math.

When you play win/lose, where you win and make a fat commission and they get hosed, you are losing about $100,000 in career referral commissions.

Win/lose is not good, not for anyone.

Go for win/win. You do this by putting their interests ahead of yours. You'll be taken care of. You'll get your commission. But don't base their buying decision on how much commission you get. Your commission has nothing to do with it.

If you get nothing else out of this book, please understand this:

If you help the prospect discover what they really want and truly need, in the price range they can afford, and you develop that reputation for the next six to twelve months, you will have more referrals than you can handle, and as much commission as you can handle.

The opposite is also true.

I am now going to insert a real life example of win/lose. I won't mention names, but I can take you to the dealership and introduce you to the salesperson in this story. The story is all too real. I have changed the names and left out the models to protect the guilty.

A salesperson related to me that he had spent over four hours with a prospect. I asked innocently, "Why so long?" The salesperson said, and I am not making this up, "The prospect wanted a _ _ _ _ _, but I wanted to sell them a _ _ _ _ _ _, and it took me that long to talk them into the _ _ _ _ _ _."

So I goes, "Why didn't you just sell them what they wanted?"

And he went, "Because I am a salesman. I don't have a swimming pool in my backyard for nothing. I made three times the commission on the _ _ _ _ _, than I would have made on the _ _ _ _ _."

Now, friends, that is win/lose, and it is why prospects do not trust salespeople.

Don't go for win/lose. If the only way you can win is for them to lose, walk away. Send them somewhere else. Better yet, go for win/win. You'll sleep better, they'll get a fair deal and you'll have more referrals than you know what to do with.

Go for win/win.

Chapter Thirty-eight

The Absolute Necessity Of Making A Fair Profit

Please do not get the idea that you should give cars and trucks away. Nothing could be further from the truth. No margin, no mission. No profit, no business. No business, no job. No job, no eat, and on and on.

If as a salesperson, you do not make a profit, you will not be a salesperson very long. If your dealership does not make a profit, it will not be a dealership very long. A fair profit for the seller is an absolute necessity, and must be obtained, or else there will be no one to supply the need for the buyer the next time.

So, how do you make a fair profit? When buyers get on the Internet and check out your invoice; when most men's and women's magazines run articles almost every month on how to buy cars; how do you make a fair profit?

Well, it begins with your belief system. If you believe that profit is a fair and necessary duty of the seller, you won't have any problems handling the prospect who tries to tell you that profit is wrong. If on the other hand you believe that profit is wrong, and that we should all be poor as church mice, you will be fair game for every prospect out there.

If you want to make a fair profit, if you want to sell at higher grosses, you need to change your belief system.

We do not see the world as it is, we see the world as we are. What we believe determines how we see the world. If your results from selling are not what you want them to be, change first what you believe. Your attitude and behavior will follow your belief.

Consider the magazine that is telling their readers that if they discover the invoice price of the vehicle they want, if they tell the dealer how much profit they are allowed to make; that if they wait until the end of the month, the salesperson will take any reasonable offer because they need a sale, and blah, blah, blah.

Do you think that the magazine which prints articles like that offers the same deal to its advertisers? Does that magazine sell their ads at invoice? Do you think the magazine tries to make a profit?

How long would a magazine stay in business if it gave away free advertising and free subscriptions? The magazines which tell your prospects that they can buy at invoice, or slightly more are simply not telling the truth, and they certainly do not practice the same things in their business.

Do not be afraid of the prospect who tells you that you don't need to make a profit. Say something like this, "I'm not sure I understand what you're trying to tell me. Is it all right if I ask you a couple of questions?

May I ask what you do for a living? Does your employer sell their goods and services at invoice? Why not? How would your employer pay wages so you could buy a car, if they made no profit on their goods and services? Do you make a profit from your work?

If you only charge your employer what it costs you to get to work, how could you afford groceries? I guess I just don't understand what you're telling me."

Your belief system must be strong enough to carry on a conversation about the necessity of profit — every time a prospect brings up the bogus idea that they can buy at invoice. They know they can't, but they read somewhere that they should use that line when they buy a car. So they do. Don't fall for it.

A fair profit is not only necessary, it is just, it is right, and it is what sets this country apart from the rest of the world. In countries where they do not believe in profit, most of the children are hungry and families live in cardboard huts. No profit means poverty, and hunger and bad water and sickness and short life spans. The next time some ill-advised prospect expects you to sell at no profit to you or the dealership, gently remind them what happens when there is no profit.

Work on your belief system.

Chapter Thirty-nine

There Are No Buying Signals

You've heard the line, "Listen for buying signals and close on them." And, "Everything they say is a buying signal."

Let's talk about that one. If you believe that there are no buying signals, you will have a much better foundation for helping the prospect get what they want, what they need and what they will pay for.

To believe in buying signals is a lot like believing in Santa Claus. If you spend all your time wishing and hoping for the prospect to say the right words, to vocalize the right buying signals, you will be constantly looking for that magic moment when the stars are right, the moon is bright, perfume fills the air and oh the night is blue ... and then they buy. Yeah, right.

If you are constantly looking for buying signals, you will not be able to pay attention to what the prospect is telling you. When you look for buying signals, you are continually planning on what closes to use next, what to say, what to do, what did they mean by that, and you will not only lose the sale, you will go nuts in the process.

It is much easier to have as a foundational belief, "There are no buying signals." That way, you are free from the worry of trying to figure out what your prospect meant by something they said, and you are free to ask questions; you are free to listen to the answers, before you begin the selling process.

In your sublime quest to find out what they really want, what they truly need, and how much they are willing to pay for it, it is much easier to ask questions and listen to the answers, rather than try to figure out where the prospect is going next, and where you will go then; there is no freedom in that kind of selling.

Free selling, that selling which comes from paying attention to the prospect, asking sincere questions, listening to the answers, not trying to find a solution until you know what the problem is — that is the kind of selling that will win the respect of the prospect, and will truly help the prospect discover for themselves what they really want, truly need and will be willing to pay for.

> There are no buying signals, only prospects who are looking for a salesperson who will shut up long enough to hear what and why and how and when and where.

Make sure you are that salesperson.

Chapter Forty

Blockbuster

By now, you should have gone to Blockbuster and rented or bought a Columbo tape.

If you have not done that yet, please put this book down, and go do it.

I'm serious.

> Learning how to listen and ask questions is the most important part of sales training.

Chapter Forty-one

No Puppy Dogs, Please

You all know about the puppy dog close. Family goes to the pet store, sees all the cute wittle puppies, but can't decide between the Great Dane or the German Shepherd.

So the salesperson says, "Hey, looks to me like the kids like this one. What say you take her home for a day or two to see how this works out?" And so the aforementioned family goes home with the cute wittle puppy. What do you think the chances are that the parents will ever bring it back? Not on your life. The kids fell in love with it. It is never coming back. Hence the 50 year old selling term, The Puppy Dog Close.

And of course you still hear it today, "Why don't you just take it home for the weekend?" or, "If you really like it, I can try to get permission for you to take it home overnight."

How about we try something a little different? How about the reverse Puppy Dog close? "Mr. Smith, I'm not sure if I should let you take this car home for the weekend. You know what will happen. You'll drive it, you'll like it, you'll fall in love with it, next thing you know, you'll want to buy it. Are you sure this is the one you really want?"

And you say those things slowly and then you wait for the answer. This way, you will know whether or not "this one" is the one they really want. If it isn't, Mr. Smith will tell you and you can start the listening process all over. Remember, your job is to help them discover what they really want, truly need, and are willing to pay for.

And yes, you're right; most prospects aren't sure themselves what they want or need. And that is why they need you.

Chapter Forty-two

Don't Use The Wheeler Which

You haven't heard of the wheeler which? Okay, so there was this guy, a sales trainer in the '50's (1950's), who came up with a way to add profit to another old fashioned American tradition, the eggnog. And if you don't know what an eggnog is, give this book to your parents. Good 'ol Elmer Wheeler came up with this clever precept, and he probably got it from his grandfather in the '90's (1890's). Down at the local hot spot, instead of the soda jerks saying, "Do you want an egg in your milkshake?" Elmer taught them to say, "Which would you prefer, one egg or two?" And this scientific line of questioning supposedly drove sales and profits through the proverbial roof.

Fifty years later, the wheeler which is still alive and well. We smugly say, "Which would you prefer, the red one or the black one?" "Is Tuesday afternoon better for you, or would you prefer Wednesday morning?" "Would you rather have the 4.9 percentage rate, or the 1.5?" And as we deliver these old lines, we think we really are coming off with some heavy selling technique.

Problem is, there is not a prospect west of the Pecos who has not heard, seen or used that close. And once prospects start recognizing your closes, they begin to look for them, and they become wary of them. And that, my friend, is when you get the silly objections. Silly objections from intelligent prospects are only a ruse to deflect the silly closes coming from the salesperson.

Do your prospects a favor. Don't use the wheeler which. If you help the prospect discover what they really want, truly need, and how much they are willing to pay to get it, those trite, old, used, redundant, diaphanous, and silly trial closes are just not necessary.

Chapter Forty-three

Don't Expect Your Prospects To Give You The Right Answers

This one is a bit tricky. In your search for information with which to help the prospect, you will need to ask questions. The question usually comes up, "What if they give me the wrong answer?"

And it is a fair question.

The answer is: there is no wrong answer. The answer you are looking for is exactly what they give you. We don't want to use questions which make us look like county prosecutors, and have the prospect end up feeling like a defendant. Prospects get enough of that at home and work.

We want to ask sincere, harmless questions which **do not** lead directly to the prospect saying yes and buying. We want our questions and the answers to lead the prospect, and the salesperson to a genuine knowledge of what the prospect wants, needs and will pay for.

So, ask every question you can think of. And don't expect easy, pat answers. Your prospect may have made up their mind to buy, but when they get to your lot, the colors, the makes and models, the endless array of choices can confuse the prospect. Do not add to that confusion by arguing with the answers you get from the prospect.

Anything they tell you is the right answer. When you are out of questions, and they are out of answers, then you take your notebook full of facts and begin to sort out those facts. As you sort them out with the prospect, you will discover together what they really want, truly need, and what they will pay for. Then you go to work and help them get it.

In real life, on your lot or in your showroom, that is as simple as it gets. The argument begins when you try to decide for the prospect what they should buy. The argument continues when you pick the price. You should not be picking those things. The prospect should be making those decisions.

If the prospect picks the vehicle, and the price, the prospect will never complain about the vehicle or the price.

CHAPTER FORTY-FOUR

Actual Columbo Questions And Statements ...

I saw these on TV, since you haven't been to Blockbuster yet, I thought I'd mention a few of these:

I don't know, ma'am
I don't understand

Gee, I shoulda thoughta that one
Uh, it's a little early for that
I don't understand
Really?
Why would you say that?

I'm willing to take all the help I can get
Why?
I'm very grateful for all the help you've given me

Gee, that's funny
Why's that?
Maybe I can pick up a few pointers

Actually there is one thing, but it probably won't make any difference
You're right
Why do you think?

There's one thing I'm not clear on
Would you go over with me once again ...
I hope you don't mind
I don't understand

Can you see the harmless, non-offensive, quiet, sincere, friendly, laid back sort of questioning and making statements?

No arm waving, no desk pounding, no theatrics, no arm wrestling, no arguing, no trial closing....

This quiet, unassuming mental state is what we are after in our selling situations.

All you have to do is go quietly about the business of helping two or three prospects every day discover what they want, what they need, why they need it, how much they are willing to pay to get it. Then help them get it.

Piece of cake.

Chapter Forty-five

Don't Look For Weaknesses In The Buyer

Selling cars is not like Sun Tzu's, The Art of War.

One of the problems with a mindset of immediate monthly numbers and units sold is looking at prospects as adversaries who must be conquered.

Terrible, terrible, terrible mistake.

A scenario where success is counted as the strong person winning and the weak person losing is not conducive to good, lasting selling practices.

When a really sophisticated buyer enters the showroom, maybe a purchasing agent, or a mechanical engineer or an accountant, they are sometimes treated differently than the little wealthy old grandma who is ready to buy.

If our belief system says that one prospect is difficult, and the other one is easy, "let's go for the easy one," then we will be tempted to take advantage of the grandma, and we may try to over-qualify the engineer, knowing that his natural resistance to purchase will be high.

Both prospects deserve the same sincere, fair, equal deal. Both prospects deserve the same undivided attention, the same discovery process, the same meeting of their wants and needs, the same full effort to sincerely help them with their purchase.

> This is more of a belief system than a technical issue. If you believe that the way to a prospect's heart is through a patient understanding of their individual wants and needs, then you will treat both prospects the same.

If you believe that you have to "make hay while the sun shines," "all is fair in love and war," "unsophisticated buyer beware," and, "I better get mine while I can," there will be a tendency for you to, as they say in court, "utilize disparate treatment."

And that will of course give you a few quick commissions, and a lot of bad reputations.

Don't look for weaknesses in a buyer and then exploit them. If you see weaknesses in a buyer, it is within your fiduciary duty to protect them, and help them, and make sure that no one takes advantage of them. They are your customers.

Fair treatment, patient questioning, taking real care of the prospect, finding out what they want, what they need and what they have allotted in their budget to pay for it, that is the belief system which will provide more repeat business than you will be able to handle.

CHAPTER FORTY-SIX

How To Sell At Prices Higher Than Your Competition

When you go out to buy something for yourself, there are many issues other than price, which will be a factor in your decision to buy.

If your gas tank is on empty in the middle of the night, in a bad part of town in a strange city, you would pay three dollars for a gallon of gas and consider yourself fortunate to find fuel.

If you were crawling through the desert, dying of thirst, needing water to keep you alive, dragging yourself over an acre of diamonds surrounded by silver dollars and gold nuggets would have no real meaning for you.

Price is relative.

Price is determined by wants. Supply and demand control the business world. Some of us feel that prices on tickets to professional football games are too high. Yet if the Browns go to the Super Bowl this year, some of us would find a way to pay $500 a ticket, plus air fare, plus hotel, plus food. Price is relative.

> The price a prospect will pay for something you are selling is dependent on how badly they want it, how badly they need it, and upon how it will meet their needs and solve their problems.

So, if you want to sell at prices higher than your competitors, it is very simple:

> Do a better job than your competitors at asking questions, listening to answers, clarifying their answers so that you understand the whole situation, and through the gentle, Columbo style of probing for information, help your prospect discover what they really want, truly need, and are willing to pay for.

And if you can do that, you will be able to sell at prices higher than your competitors. Why? Because your competition, in a rush to get the sale, are ignoring the prospect's wants, they are trial closing them, they are offending them, they are hammering them, and by doing those things, your competition is sending their prospects to you.

Your competition is forcing their prospects to raise their defenses, fight back and resist buying. And the worse the prospect is being treated, the more places they will shop.

Price is relative. Wants are important. Needs are important. Likes are important. Desires are important. Everything the prospect says is important.

Find out what your prospects really want, truly need and are willing to pay for, and then help them get it. If you do that, you will smoke the competition so bad they will beg for your secrets, offer you a job, bribe you, and etcetera.

Price is relative.

Information from the prospect is priceless.

CHAPTER FORTY-SEVEN

Everything The Prospect Says Is Important

Let the prospect talk. Get them to talk. When they stop talking, ask more questions. Let them say anything they want to say.

Remember that no one listens to them. No one compliments them. No one lets them say two words without interrupting them.

Never interrupt them.

Everything the prospect says is important. It is important to them. What they say has meaning for them. It may not be what you think or feel, but it is what they think and feel. Therefore it is important.

Listen, understand, take notes on everything they say. They will give you all the information you need to help them, if you just be quiet and listen to them.

Don't correct them when they make a mistake. They are allowed to make a mistake without being corrected by a salesperson. Don't let an inherent need to be right keep you from making a sale. Don't correct them. Don't try to make sure that they see things the same way you do. They don't. They are the prospect. They have the right to see things any way they want to.

When the prospect says something with which you do not agree, you can correct them, straighten them out, tell them off, or you can let it go and make the sale.

You can be right, or you can make the sale and spend the commission. You get no commission when you correct the prospect, and make them feel like two cents.

You can be right, or you can make the sale. You can rarely do both.

Chapter Forty-eight

Sell Them What They Want

I shouldn't have to include this chapter, but I am going to. This page is as important as anything in this book. Remember, we are focusing on the prospect, what they want, what they need, what they will pay for.

I have a great idea: how about we sell them what they want? How about we stop switching them to another vehicle with higher sticker and more commission?

> Do you want to know why most prospects leave your lot without buying? ***Because you won't sell them what they want.*** That's right. You won't sell them what they want.

You won't let them buy what they want.

You're always trying to sell them what **you want to sell them**, what you want them to buy.

So they walk.

And they go to your competition. You do the math.

How smart is that for you? How much commission do you make when they go to the competition?

Your prospects do not have the same likes, dislikes, wants and needs as you do. They have their own wants and needs.

A prospect comes in your showroom and tells you which vehicle they want. And immediately you think you can switch them either to a vehicle you need to move, or a vehicle which carries more commission, or a higher priced vehicle.

And they walk.

Gee, Sherlock, I wonder why. It doesn't take a detective to figure this one out. You are ignoring their wants; you are telling them that what they want is not important, that you know more than they do.

> Sell them what they want. If you ignore everything else in this book, and just sell them what they tell you they want, you can double your sales.

Find out what they want. Sell them what they want.

Prospects will not object to what they want, in the price range they can afford.

It is not rocket science. Sell them what they want.

Chapter Forty-nine

Stop With The "Bump"

We all know what the bump is. That is where the prospect says, "I would like to be somewhere around the 350 a month range." And when the sale is all done, they are at 417.50 a month.

Can you say, "Hosed"?

Let's be real. Stop bumping them. It is not your money. You don't have to make the payments. It is not your financial future. It is theirs, and if you are far enough along in the process to discuss their finances, then you are in a fiduciary relationship to them. You owe them trust and complete honesty.

If they told you that they want to be in the 350.00 range, it is your duty to put them into something in the 350.00 range. Period. 400.00 is not in the 350.00 range. It may be your range, but it is not theirs.

Honest selling.

Honest selling.

Honest selling.

Sell them what they want in the price range they can afford. If you do this, you will get more referrals than anyone in town. You won't be able to do the paperwork. You will make more money. You will sell more cars. You can take more trips and buy more stuff. You can play more golf. Fish more. Whatever. Sell them what they want in the price range they tell you they want to be in.

This is honest selling. The theme of this little book is that we ask questions, we listen, we help the prospect discover what they really want and truly need, and what they are willing to pay for. And we do not take advantage of the prospect. And we close the deal by selling them what they want and need, in the price range they want to pay. That is honest selling. If you do that, you won't be able to handle the business by yourself.

Stop with the bump. If they want to spend more, they will tell you. If they want to bump themselves, that is their right, but it is not your right. Now here is a newsflash. The biggest reason why we should stop the bump is this:

When they pick the vehicle, they will not object to the vehicle.

When they pick the price, they will not object to the price.

Just think of it, no objections, either on the vehicle or the price. And what did we do to be so blessed? We let them tell us what they want, what they need and how much they are willing to pay.

How smooth is that?

How easy is that?

It is literally, and figuratively, a piece of cake.

Why don't you just tell them during the initial meeting and greeting stage that you really don't know what they want or need yet, and in order to find that out, you will need to ask some questions; and that your only goal in the selling process is to help them get what they want in the price range they want to pay?

Better carry some smelling salts, they'll probably faint. Prospects aren't used to being treated like that. They are used to the strong arm tactics, the closes, the traps, the pressure.

This step is so simple. Let them tell you. Stop telling them. Let them pick the price. Stop picking it for them. They already know what they want and can afford. It is so easy, I can't believe there is a chapter on it.

CHAPTER FIFTY

Stop Rushing The Prospect

More prospects would drive on your lot during daylight hours if they could just look at cars and trucks for a few minutes before being body checked.

This is not hockey.

This is not barrel racing.

This is not calf roping.

This is people, who have jobs, who want to look at the object of their desire for a few minutes on their way to work, to church, to the ball game, to the restaurant. But they don't stop then because they know that a salesperson will rush them, do the dog and pony show, and frankly, the prospect doesn't have time.

So they stop after you are closed. They can't get T.O.'d after working hours.

So let the prospect look around. Give them some time. Don't rush them. Do you like to be rushed when you are shopping? Do you enjoy someone with commission breath following you around, trying to talk you into buying something before you are ready?

Give them some time. It is our own fault that the lot is full of lookers after closing time. Sunday afternoons may be the only time your prospects can look without being chased down.

We are making it so that if they want to look at cars, they have to do it after we are closed. The sad thing is that the owner spends millions on inventory, thousands on blacktop and concrete, lights, streamers, clean-up............and when a prospect pulls on the lot, we won't let them look at anything.

Actually, it is worse than that. The first thing we try to do is to get them away from our million dollar inventory, and into our ninety-nine dollar desk; next to our salesman of the month plaques; so they can see our awards.

What is wrong with this picture?

It is us. It is we. It is I. It is our fault. For pete's sake, let them look already.

Now here is the way we can turn this around. This month, instead of spending 30 to 50 thousand dollars trying to get prospects to visit your dealership, consider the ad on the following page:

To our valued customers and friends: As of this date, we want you to feel free to browse our lot and look at the selection of new and used vehicles we have in stock.

Our salespeople have clear instructions to let you look as long as you want to. Several of our customers have stated that the only time they can freely look at our vehicles is after we are closed. That is our fault.

From now on, we will give you all the time you want to look at our vehicles, during daylight, during working hours.

We will not interrupt you until you need help. If you are not able to look until you are content, call me personally at ____________________.

Thank you for your business.

Signed______________________________

Can you imagine the response?

Can you imagine how the competition will feel?

Can you imagine how you will feel when the competition, all of them, copy your advertisement?

This is not rocket science. Prospects want to look. So let them look.

Run the ad for a full month, then for another month. The money you save could be used for, say, training for salespeople and managers, or for fishing, or for golf, or for bonuses, or whatever.

Sincerity, honesty, helping, listening, discovering, helping the prospect discover their own wants and needs, this is real selling in the real world to real people with real needs.

If you do it, you won't be able to handle the referrals. Really.

Chapter Fifty-one

Sales Is Not A Numbers Game

This is another selling myth from the dark ages of selling back when coke was still cola, a joint was a bad place to be and Merle Haggard still had a full head of hair. This myth is still being perpetuated by people who should know better. As long as we look to the end of this month's numbers as the measure of success or failure in selling, it will be difficult to stop looking at sales as a numbers game.

Sales is not a numbers game. Sales is a people business.

When your prospects get a twitch of an inkling of a feeling that you might consider treating them like a number, that sales process is over. Roy Orbison over. Your prospect doesn't love you any more, over. It's over.

The one thing which always comes out in your first five minutes with the prospect is the prospect's understanding of whether or not you are treating them like a person, or a number.

Consider the manager who still tells you that sales is a numbers game. Manager says, "The more prospects you see, the more money you will make." That may be true unless you are treating the prospects like they are just numbers. You can talk to fifty prospects a day, and if you treat them all like numbers, like cattle, you're just not going to sell much. Consider also the old line, "Selling is nothing but the law of averages." Yeah, right. The law of averages is not all that clear either. If you put one foot in a bucket of Pepsi, and the other in a bucket of Coca Cola, on the average, you would probably not drink from either bucket.

In real selling, where your job is to help the prospect discover what they really want, truly need, and what they are willing to pay to get it, the only law of averages you ever need to concern yourself with is this one:

> If you use the selling methods of the average automobile salesperson, you will always sell what the average automobile salesperson sells.

If you are treating your prospects like sales is a numbers game, you will never be able to rise above the heap of mediocre salespeople.

HR rule: prospects do not like to be treated like numbers.

HR rule for sales managers: salespeople do not like to be treated like numbers.

One thing I have noticed about sales managers who think that sales is a numbers game, they spend all their time hiring and firing. They wonder why their salespeople have no repeat business. And these sales managers can't keep salespeople, any more than their salespeople can keep customers. If you are a sales manager and you think that turnover of salespeople is expensive, think what it is costing you to turn all of those prospects over to your competition. Who did you think you were turning them over to? Mr. Rogers?

Customer turnover means no repeat business.

If we believe that sales is a numbers game, it means that we are prone to treat prospects like cattle. Head 'em up, move 'em out. Hint, hint: people do not like being treated like cattle. Remember the scenes from the old westerns when the herd was rounded up, unbranded cattle cut from the herd, brought to the blazing fire, thrown to the ground and branded with a red-hot branding iron? That scene is reminiscent of most closing techniques at dealerships where salespeople and prospects are treated like cattle.

Prospects are not cattle.

Prospects are not numbers.

Prospects are people and sales is not a numbers game.

Prospects are people with feelings and wants and needs and hopes and dreams for the future. When these people enter your lot or showroom, they become prospects who have wants and needs, and they know about how much they will pay for those wants and needs.

Sales is not a numbers game. Sales is a necessary transaction in a civilized society where the seller must learn what the buyer really wants, truly needs and how much the buyer will pay to get it.

This is not rocket science.

If selling has become very difficult for you, it could be that you have bought into the false line that selling is a numbers game.

It is not.

> If you treat prospects like cattle, they will stampede to your competition. If, however, your competition treats prospects like cattle, you, dear reader, who are learning to treat prospects like people, can double or triple your personal best in selling.

Fishing is a numbers game. Basketball is a numbers game. Math is a numbers game. Selling is a people business.

Chapter Fifty-two

Stop Trying To Control The Sale

If you once believed that sales is a numbers game, then you may be working under the false assumption that you can control the sales process.

You cannot.

If you think that you can control prospects, what you will end up with is a few sales each month from people who were compliant enough to be manipulated by aggressive sales tactics. Problem is that there just isn't enough of those passive/compliant prospects around to keep your sales where you want them to be.

You cannot control the sales process.

Controlling the sale is old-school thinking. It does not work in today's educated society. In reality, it probably never worked, but before television and the Internet, some salespeople and trainers thought it did.

So they tried it, and taught it, and the belief is still around.

> The salesperson who thinks that he can control the sale is quite possibly driving everyone away whom he cannot control. By trying to control the sales process, that salesperson is sending qualified prospects directly to the competition. Do the math. It's not pretty.

The manager who thinks that he can control salespeople, and that salespeople can control the sales process will spend half his time hiring new salespeople. And when the salespeople quit, where do they go? That's right, to the competition. So, not only are the salespeople chasing prospects to the competition, the manager is chasing salespeople directly to the competition. How much do you think that is costing the dealership? There is a solution.

STOP TRYING TO CONTROL THE SALES PROCESS.

If you are going to try to control the sales process, you must first control the prospect. But prospects are people. People have wants and needs and likes and dislikes. If you attempt to control them in any way, they are going straight from your lot to the competition.

Think about it for a second. Do you like someone trying to control you? Do you like being told, "Sit here." "Stand there." "Go over there." "Follow me." "No, you can't look at the car yet." Put yourself in the position of the prospect. How do you feel when you buy things? Do you like being controlled? Do you like being told what you should buy, why you should buy it, when you should buy it, how you should pay for it, whether or not you should undercoat it or buy an extended warranty for it?

Of course you don't. You're human. You're a person. You're an American. Nobody tells us what we have to do or not do. That very idea is offensive to us. Have you ever wondered why the majority of prospects walk out of your showroom without buying?

Because this is a free country. They don't have to buy from you.

They will only buy from you if they want to buy from you.

You can't make them buy from you with control tactics.

Matter of fact, the more you try to control these free people, the faster they will go somewhere else. Do the math. You may be making your competition rich.

The dictionary defines control as the act of "... exercising authority over, directing, commanding...," "... the power to direct or regulate."

Now let's be honest with each other. How many people in your life can you exercise authority over? How many people in your life are you able to direct and command? How many people are you directing or regulating?

We all know the answer to those questions. Not very many. There may be people that you THINK you can control and command, but we know what happens when you try it.

Hey, wake up. This is America. We don't like to be controlled. We don't like to be T.O.'d. We don't like to be bumped. We don't like to be high pressured. We don't like to be flim-flammed. We don't trust fast talking politicians and we sure don't like fast talking salespeople.

The controlling the sale thing was over a long time ago. So, you might better give it up. You might want to give up your need to control things long enough to pay attention to your prospect.

If you really must control things, get a dog. I know, get a Great Pyrenees. A male will be nice. Try to control him for a year or two. Call me and let me know how it works out. If you want a real challenge, here it is: Control yourself. Control your urge to control the prospect. Give up all control to the prospect. Find out what they want. Listen to what they need. Discover how much they want to pay. Then let them buy what they want, need and are willing to pay for.

The real control is no control. Give up your personal, ego-driven need to control your prospects. You can't control them anyway. The only sale you will ever control is the sale in which you give up control to the prospect.

Let the prospect control the sale. That way, all you need to worry about is:

Finding out what they really want;

Finding out what they really need;

Finding out how much they are willing to pay to get it.

Three simple steps, but if you try to control the sale by controlling the prospect, they will not tell you what they want, what they need, or how much they are willing to pay to get it.

Really, seriously, please, listen: prospects are people. They cannot be controlled. Their upbringing will not allow it. They have been taught all their lives that this is a free country, and we are allowed to make our own decisions. Give up. Let them do what they believe is their right. Go back to page one of this book and start over. This entire book is about giving up control and listening to your prospect. Give up control. Help your prospect vocalize what they want, need and will pay for.

There are just not enough people in the country who want YOU to control them and their buying decisions. Give it up. Find out what they want, need, and are willing to pay for. Then help them get it. That is all the control you will ever need.

CHAPTER FIFTY-THREE

The Secret To Selling

There is a secret to selling. I saved it for last, hoping that the foundation in the preceding chapters has prepared you to receive, accept and incorporate this secret to sales success.

When you read the secret, read it again, and again, and again. Read the secret until you know it backwards and forwards, until it is as common to your thought process as breathing is to your lungs. Memorize this secret until you can use it as easily as writing your name. This secret must become a part of your conscious and sub-conscious awareness. You will need to be able to use the secret without even thinking about it.

Here is the secret:

People will pay more for what they want, less for what they need, and much less for what they don't want or need.

And as Ray Charles once said, "One more time now" —

People will pay more for what they want;

Less for what they need;

And much less for what they don't want or need.

The reason why sales is so hard for most salespeople is because most of their time is taken up with trying to sell prospects something they do not want or need. And prospects will resist products that they do not want or need. At the very least, prospects who do not want or need the products will object to the price, and object to the price, and object to the price.

Prospects just won't pay much for things they don't want or need.

The only argument that a prospect has when they don't want or need something is to get the price down as low as possible. If they don't want it or need it, they will still buy it, if the price is right, you know, below invoice, no commission. Sales managers like to call those "mini-deals." Nothing but an inventory mover, no profit, just problems.

The average salesperson in the average dealership begins his sales career this way:

1. answers an ad in the paper
2. dresses up and goes to the interview
3. is hired by the manager
4. has a couple of days to learn to meet and greet
5. has a few days to learn to qualify the prospect
6. couple of days to learn the product presentation
7. the manager will close the deals

In this brief introductory period, there is no real sales training. No one tells the new salesperson the secret to selling. No one bothers to tell the new salesperson that prospects will pay more for what they want, less for what they need, and much less for what they don't want or need.

And so our hero spends all his time trying to sell the prospects what he thinks they want. Our hero gets shut down time after time. Said hero keeps trying to talk prospects into buying what he thinks they need. In a couple of weeks, our hero gets lucky and sells one to his uncle. Hero sells another to his old football coach. Hero then does a mini-deal for his mother-in-law. In the meantime, twenty or thirty other prospects walk, and after a few dismal weeks, our aforementioned hero quits, having sold four or five units to family and friends.

Hence the ad in the newspaper every other week, run by a manager who can't manage, train, hire, or prepare salespeople for the real world of selling.

It is all quite simple when we know the secret. The key to a prospect's heart is to find out what they want. The old selling fable, "Find a need and fill it," is not the whole story. The whole story is, "Find a want and fill it." That is much closer to the truth. Prospects will talk about what they want. It is more difficult to get them to talk about what they need.

It is much more difficult to get them to talk about how much they are willing to pay to get what they want and need. But oh, how they will go on about what they want, and what they like. But no one told our hero that, so he bombed out of sales. Who knows, with the right training, our hero could be selling 30 cars a month, with good grosses. But no one bothered to tell him the secret.

Here is the secret once more:

People will pay more for what they want;

Less for what they need;

And much less for what they don't want or need.

How does that apply to us? Well, like this:

When a prospect pulls on your lot or walks into your showroom, they have only one basic transportation need. Their only basic need is to get from point A to point B. THAT IS THEIR ONLY BASIC TRANSPORTATION NEED. PERIOD. One very basic need.

But, there are about 1,000 variations on what they **want** to get them from point A to point B. There is style, comfort, color, luxury and hundreds of other accessories. These other things make up what they want.

So, for the first fifteen or twenty minutes, why don't we talk about what they want, why they want it, what will happen if they don't get it, how long have they wanted it, what have they done to get it, where else are they going and what else are they going to do until they find what they want?

If you ask about everything, and listen to the answers, and take notes on what they say, they will talk until the cows come home. And after they have told you everything, and you have listened and taken good notes, **they** will have a better understanding of what **they** want. When they drove on your lot, they may not have been sure. But now, after you let them talk about what they want, they now understand what they want, and you helped them to understand that. And when they understand that you understand them, they begin to trust you.

Only when they trust you, do you then begin to ask about what they need, and why, and when, and how, and where. Same process, you ask questions, take notes, they give the answers. Once again, you help them understand what it is they need. When **they** understand what **they** need, they begin to trust you.

Only when they trust you, when they have told you what they want and need, <u>then</u> you help them to discover how much they are willing to pay for what they want and need.

When you by sincere, patient, gentle questioning have uncovered those three closely guarded secrets:

1. what they want and why
2. what they need and why
3. how much they will pay and why

then and only then, are you in a position to sell them what they want, need, and are willing to pay for.

Where is the pressure? There is none. Where are the trial closes? They are not necessary. Where is the control of the sale? It is with the prospect. Where is the adversarial relationship between normal car buyer and car salesperson? It does not exist. Where is the need for the bump? There is no need. Where is the arguing over price? There is no arguing over price. The prospect picked the price. Where are the objections? There are none. The prospect picked the vehicle, and the price.

This process is the goose that lays the golden eggs. And if you don't kill the goose, that goose will lay a golden egg every day, right in the middle of your desk. And when you get used to the goose laying a gold egg right in the middle of your desk every day, pretty soon, you'll get two gold eggs a day, one in the morning, and one in the afternoon. You know what that translates into?

Forty cars a month.

You will need a secretary, and another bank to put your money in.

If you find out those three things, in that order,

What they want and why
What they need and why
How much they are willing to pay and why,

They will pressure you to sell to them. It is human nature. They know what they want, you helped them discover what they want, and you have what they want. They will pressure you to get it.

So don't learn to handle objections. There are too many of them. Learn instead to sell without getting objections. It is so much easier.

Here is the secret again: People will pay more for what they want, less for what they need, and much less for what they don't want or need.

And in every dealership in America, every day, every week, every month, this is how it plays out:

Amateur salespeople try to sell a prospect what they neither want or need.

Average salespeople try to sell a prospect what they need.

Professional salespeople sell a prospect what they want.

It is simple. It is not all that easy at first. But it is that simple. Just listen, ask questions, don't argue with the prospect. The prospect is a person, just like us. They think like us, they have feelings like we do, they want the same things we want. Just find out what they want and help them get it.

Just find out
what they want
and
help them get it.

So you are at the end of the book.

Now what?

Are you going to change the way you see yourself and the way you see your customers? Or are you going to revert back to the same way everyone else is doing it?

The car business is changing. Customers are changing. Sales is changing. The market is changing. The world economy is changing.

The dealership, the managers and the salespeople who do not change with the times will find it very hard to keep up.

If you need help with implementing the changes in this book, call me at 1.800.380.3040 and we can talk about it.

Thanks for buying the book.

J.B.